LETTERS
FROM DAD

LETTERS FROM DAD

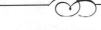
lessons and love

JOHN BROOME
with
JACK BROOME

WARNER BOOKS

A Time Warner Company

Some names and identifying details, including the names of Jack's classmates at the Cate School, have been changed in order to protect the privacy of individuals involved.

Warner Books, Inc., 1271 Avenue of the Americas, New York, NY 10020

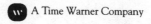 A Time Warner Company

First Warner Books printing: May 1996
10 9 8 7 6 5 4 3 2 1

Library of Congress Cataloging-in-Publication Data

Broome, John
    Letters from dad: lessons and love/ John Broome with Jack Broome.
        p.   cm.
    ISBN 0-446-52014-4
    1. Broome, John, 1940—Correspondence.   2. Broome, Jack 1976—Correspondence.   3. Fathers—United States—Correspondence.
4. Fathers and sons—United States—Case studies.   I. Broome, Jack, 1976–   .   II. Title.
HQ756.B74   1996
306.874'2—dc20
                                                                                    95-47581
                                                                                        CIP

Book design by Giorgetta Bell McRee

FOREWORD

When I stepped into the dining room, my father was standing there with tears in his eyes. I knew at once that these were tears of joy. He stepped toward me, gave me a smile, and threw his arms around me. I'll never forget the feeling I had as the chills went through my body. Then my dad turned and pointed to the dining room table. Looking over, I saw the two opened letters sitting side by side on the table, one from Thacher School and one from Cate School.

My dad had introduced me to the idea of going away to boarding school when I was in fifth grade and I had been intent on doing it from that point on. I knew that in such a competitive world I had to get the best education possible, and in the end I'd have no choice but to leave Fresno to go to a boarding school. After every report card, my dad and I would sit down and talk about how I was doing and what I had to do in order to get the grades to be accepted to the schools of my choice.

I didn't even need to read the letters across the room, since I could see that the first word on both of them was "Congratulations." That was all that I needed. It was like a dream. Speechless, I hugged my dad again. I will never forget the look on his face and the tears in his eyes when I walked in the door that day.

My dad left the decision as to which school up to me. He said I had earned the right to choose. And, after we revisited Cate and Thacher, I picked Cate. Well, I had reached my first goal. All of the years of hard work in grammar school had paid off, and I was going off to boarding school.

But it was not until late in the summer before freshman year that I realized how hard it was going to be to leave home. My dad and I had been best friends since I was a young boy, and by eighth grade, we were inseparable. We did just about everything together. When I was young we went to the zoo together many weekends, and when we weren't out doing something like that, I would sit for hours with him in his study while he worked.

Then, when I was about eleven years old, my parents got divorced. Let me tell you, divorce isn't a fun thing for a kid to deal with. I found out about it one day when my dad picked me up from a friend's house. Instead of going straight home, my dad passed the house and parked in an olive orchard down the road. It was then that he told me a divorce was imminent. I was crushed. The safe, stable world I had grown accustomed to seemed to be collapsing all around me. All that I could do was trust my dad when he told me that everything would turn out all right.

When my dad moved out of our house, it wasn't long before I went to live with him. It was during the years of living together that my dad and I became even closer. We spent every evening and almost every weekend together. I accompanied him to many of his business meetings and dinners, and was always included in the conversation. My dad really seemed to listen to my ideas. On weekends, we would go shooting together or just hop in the car and head for some adventure in the mountains. But no matter what it was we were doing, my dad always found some lesson in it for me. The business meetings, the drives (we called them adventures), they all had an objective. Even the chores that my dad made me do every day around the house had a purpose. I didn't get paid for my chores because my dad had taught me that to be part of the household, it was my responsibility to do my fair share to keep things together. I didn't realize it at the time, but in the years that we lived alone together, my dad was doing everything that he could to teach me what the world is really like.

When the time came to head off to Cate School, I really didn't know what to think or what to take or even exactly what to wear. My dad and I weren't very happy about the idea of being separated. As I packed, my cat, Frazzle, seemed to sense a change coming and became more hysterical by the day.

Although my dad did not really want to see me go, he knew that I had to go. His first concern had always been my best interest, and he knew that going away to school was the best thing for me. The time had come for me to take everything that he had taught me and put it into practice, to do a bit of growing by myself. I was only a fourteen-year-old kid from Fresno (and I was scared), but the challenge excited me.

When my dad brought me to Cate and the time came to say good-bye, he said something that seemed strange at the time. "Jack," he said, "I think that it will be better if I don't write you for a few weeks. I want to give you time to really settle in and get used to being away at school." Well, he was telling the truth. For about three weeks I did not receive any letters from my dad. We talked on the phone a few times, but that was it.

I really began to miss the communication, so I called and asked my dad to write me. Bang! That was all it took. The letters started coming. Every other day or so I received one. My friends thought it was hilarious. They thought that it was even funnier when they saw that some of the letters began with sentences like "Let's talk about death," "Let's talk about sex," or "Let's talk about politics." Then some of my close friends began asking to read Dad's letters. And I realized they were something very special.

These letters have been the primary way that my dad and I have kept up our relationship in my four years away at Cate. I should have known that my dad would find a way to keep in touch and keep teaching me. Every letter that he sent me took on a new issue. If I was having a problem with something, my dad would write me a letter of advice on how I might deal with it. If I did not understand something, he would write me a letter explaining whatever it was that I could not understand. And if I was doing just fine, he would use his letters to encourage me to keep it up, to catch me up on current events at home, and to generally explain some of the many different aspects of his life to me.

For the first few months, adjusting to Cate was the main topic of most of my dad's letters. Once I had settled in, the letters became more teaching instruments than anything else. My dad and I talked on the phone every couple of nights, but my dad put the meat of what he wanted to talk to me about in letters. This probably made more sense, because sometimes I had to reread his letters several times over before I really understood what he was trying to explain.

For me it was different. I had no problem getting everything off my mind with my dad on the phone. I just didn't have the time or really the ability to put all of my thoughts onto paper. Sometimes my dad had trouble understanding this, but I really think he understood more than he let on. He got very frustrated at the fact that I rarely sent letters. At first he said he thought that I just didn't appreciate his letters and that I wasn't taking the time to absorb what he wrote. He couldn't have been more wrong. It was because of his letters that my dad and I remained so close even after I left home. Because we could no longer spend as much time together as we had when I was home, it was the letters that kept us close. I treasured every letter as if it were a part of me.

Then, halfway through my sophomore year, my dad was involved in a double-fatality accident, broadsided at an intersection by a drunk driver. Seeing him lying in a hospital bed all cut up and with a broken neck, I thought that I was going to lose the most important thing in the world to me. In fact, the first time I saw him, I actually passed out.

It was only after almost losing him that I truly realized how much my dad meant to me. I took some time off from school in order to stay at home and take care of my dad. I did things for him that he had done for me when I was little, like bathing him and helping him go to the toilet. For the following year, he had trouble remembering some things. It was not until Christmas break of my junior year that he finally seemed to be operating as his old self.

Looking back on the accident, it was a huge growing experience in our relationship. All that my dad had tried to tell me about mortality became fully clear. Without a doubt, my dad and I came to really appreciate life, and each other, much more after the accident.

Now, at the end of my high-school career, it is amazing to think back at how different I am now from when I first left home. For almost four years, my dad's letters have kept me on track and helped me to mature. I keep the letters from each year in separate shoe boxes in my room at home. They mean more to me than any material thing I have. They are the guidelines that have gone so far to make up the person that I am today.

—Jack Broome

FRESHMAN
YEAR

9/3/91

Dear Jack,

After almost fifteen years, the last four living in a man's world with your dad, you're now on your own. Now you get to use all the values and lessons that you have learned. I have every confidence in you, son, *you're a winner!*

I send you off to Cate with a heavy heart. . . . I will miss you so much. But I also send you off with the joy of a father who has tried his best to provide his son with a solid foundation for his life and has seen his son thrive under every challenge and opportunity. I know that boarding school will be no different.

I love you, Jack, I'm behind you all the way. Be serious, work hard, play hard, and have fun. Make friends by being a friend.

Love

Dad

9/26/91

Dear Jack,

It's hard to believe that you've been at Cate for *four* weeks. Almost a month has gone by so quickly!! I miss you a lot; so does Frazzle. She almost had a complete breakdown the first 10 days you were gone!!

I know you've been busy and adjusting to being away at school but I do hope you'll get in the habit of calling frequently, even just to say "hi" and let me know that all is well. And from time to time *write* to share your thoughts and experiences.

I'm planning the 5th with Derek and Steph to take you out to dinner and celebrate your birthday. We'll go out to dinner and whatever you would like. Sunday morning we can shop at Nordstrom's if you like, then leave about 1:00.

On Parents' Weekend Jan and I are planning to arrive Friday morning the 18th and stay to Sunday. Bob may stop in to have dinner with us. . . . Let me know what the schedule for Parents' Weekend is.

You are due for a weekend at home either Nov. 2–3, 9–10, or 16–17. Let me know which dates you would prefer (Derek & Steph will be here 2–3 and 16–17) and let me know if there is anything special you would like to do.

I have made airplane reservations for you to come home November 26th for Thanksgiving and return to school December 3rd. The reservations had to be made 30 days in advance and only cost $120 round trip.

Not much news from home. I'm home all week trying to catch up on work I've delayed the last several weeks

I've been going to Florida. Nothing very special going on. I'm anxious to hear about your outing at Catalina. Call me when you get back.

    Much Love
        Dad

10/10/91

Dear Jack,

I can't tell you how good it was to see you last weekend. . . . You have matured in just the one month you have been away . . . you looked so happy and fit . . . you made me proud!!

I was greatly impressed with the caliber of your schoolmates. They all seem to be bright and good-natured. I noticed the tremendous amount of mutual support they seem to give each other. You might pay a bit more attention yourself to this fact. (I'm not criticizing you, just a friendly suggestion.) I noticed most of your teammates complimenting you on your play, particularly when you made a point (i.e., "Jack, you're awesome"). You might ask yourself how many times *you* complimented or encouraged your teammates. How many pats on the back *you* gave. Remember, to have a friend, you have to be a friend.

I agree with your idea of not coming home for a "long weekend" before Thanksgiving . . . 3:00 Friday to 6:00 Sunday, with the eight-hour drive to get you here and return (16 hours for me) leaves little time for what[ever—ed.]. . . . Frazzle would be mad as hell if she knew your decision. So pick a weekend & I'll come down & we'll spend the time in LA and Santa Barbara. Perhaps dinner with Bob can be included. So the weekend of . . .

Oct 26–27 (maybe w/ D&S)
Nov 2–3 (w/ D&S)
Nov 9–10 (w/ just me)
Nov 16–17 (w/ D&S)

If it's a weekend with Derek & Steph then I'll be down to pick you up at 8:00 P.M. Friday; if it's *just* me, I'll be down at 3:30 P.M. All in all I'd prefer the 9th and 10th. Let me know what you'd like & what you would like to do that weekend.

Not much news here that you don't already know. Bob brought us a numbered print of his wife's painting of the coast. He took it back to have it framed for us. I gave Ben an envelope for you (your plane ticket for Thanksgiving, some Tegrin, etc.) and he said he would bring it to you next weekend. Speaking of Ben, he said he gave you the photos of you "cowboying." Save them or send them to me, I'd like to see them.

I've enclosed two items for you to read. The article on manners is important. Please save it & return it to me.

I love you very much and I miss you more than you know but I'm proud of what you're doing & support you all the way.

Dad

10/15/91

Dear Jack,

I've been so worried about *you* adjusting to being away at school that I forgot to realize that it might be *me* that had to adjust.

All the time we were talking about your going to boarding school *my* mind's eye envisioned you coming home most weekends. I really didn't envision a life so separated from you as it now appears the next four years will be. I understand your desire to stay at Cate weekends and I think all the sports activities and camaraderie at Cate is wonderful. *But* I do miss our talks and the ability to have a profound influence on your thinking and maturing.

I wanted you to have influences to broaden you and other role models to make you a better rounded person. But I do want to insure some impact from your sainted father.

So if it can't always be there in person then it will have to be by mail. I'll just have to put into letters what we would have talked about were we together each night. So count on receiving some letters of substance from time to time. And I hope you will *really read* them and answer them.

Years ago, I used to go to the trade show each year in Chicago while I was president of Alpine Equipment Co. The first year the chap in the booth opposite ours had his young son (10–11 years old) with him. The boy was fidgety and bored, but he listened while his dad explained things to him. The next year the boy was more mature, had grown 3–4 inches and watched all that went on attentively. The next year the boy had glasses, had grown another 2–3 inches, and his dad had him passing out literature in the aisle. The last year I was there the boy was selling under the watchful eye of his dad. His dad was teaching him all he knew and preparing him for his life ahead. I was always impressed with that and swore I would be as good a dad to my son.

So plan to get some letters, Jack. I'm no Lord Chesterfield but I'll try.

And were something to ever happen to me, I'll never regret on my deathbed that there were so many things I wanted to tell you but was going to wait until "later" when we "had more time" and it was "more convenient."

Dad

10/20/91

Dear Jack,

As I left you yesterday, you said, "This is supposed to be sad." *Wrong!* You're strong, you're happy, you have entered a new stage in your life, with new friends, new challenges, new inspirations, and that's great. That's what's right for a young man of fifteen. That's why I encouraged you to go to boarding school.

And that's why I'm *honored* to pay your way. You've earned your place at Cate and it's yours. And that makes me *happy*. Sure, I miss you. And sure, I enjoy your company and wish you were here. And sure, I'd love to spend a *week* with you or stay as close as Andy's mother does. But that would defeat the purpose of your being at Cate. So when we say "good-bye," I'm happy . . . for you, for what you've earned, for where you are, for what you're becoming, and for my feelings of pride for my son.

I got a kick out of your answering my question, in the car, before I had gotten three words out of my mouth. Yes, Jack, we are close. Two weeks ago, you said, "It seems like I just saw you an hour ago." (It had been a month.) That's what happens when two people are as close as we are. . . . And *that* makes me proud.

Boy, it's a good thing I left early. The "grapevine" was one big traffic jam from Magic Mountain to Gorman, with people going to see "the umbrellas."* After Gorman it got a little better down to the bottom of the hill, but not much. You can't believe the number of people

---

*Fifteen hundred large yellow umbrellas placed around Tejon Pass by the artist Christo, who created "Running Fence" in Sonoma County and draped the islands near Palm Beach in pink.

who were there, sitting under umbrellas, tak[
wandering around, etc. And what made it worse wa~ ~
the cars that had to stop due to overheating. Anyway, it
was a mess . . . and a friend of mine came in three hours
later from LA and she said it was *much* worse.

Bad news . . . Mark Barsotti broke his leg in Friday
night's game. Fresno was ranked 21 in the nation and
Barsotti was up for the Heisman Trophy. He will be out
for six weeks and a redshirt *freshman* will take over!! I
don't know how it will affect his nomination for the
Heisman, but it can't help. He broke it on a scramble
when the team was ahead 28–7. (Dumb!!!!)

I'll do your wash this week and send it down with
your mother when I pick Derek & Stephanie up Friday
afternoon.

I called Andreas & told him that he really ought to
get his parents to take him for a visit to Cate but if he
couldn't I'd bring him with me when I come to Cate
next time. I hope that's OK.

I've enclosed a little piece for you to read. The honor
part doesn't apply to you, you're honorable, but the part
about "everybody does it" might be something to think
about. The point being, *march to the beat of your own
drummer*. Do what *you* know is right, *not what everybody
else does*.

Try to get along with Henry. He is self-centered and
spoiled, but consider your source, count your blessings
(you have been raised with different values), and try to
get along with him. Maybe, though he would never
admit it, you can teach him a thing or two and he will
appreciate it.

That's about it for now. (*60 Minutes* is about to start.)

. . . Read Wm. Prince's little book on Curtis Wolsey Cate and tell me what you think. And find out for me what Cate's connection with Thacher School was?? And can you believe Mr. Daniel not recognizing you!!! That blows me away. I would have rather hoped he would have looked you up. Oh well.

I'll post this now. Much love, great son . . . you'll make it to a great college, believe me . . . and *never, never* lower your sights.

> Love
>
> Dad

"IT'S O.K., SON, EVERYBODY DOES IT"
BY JACK GRIFFIN

When Johnny was six years old, he was with his father when they were caught speeding. His father handed the officer a five-dollar bill with his driver's license. "It's O.K., Son," his father said as they drove off. "Everybody does it."

When he was eight, he was permitted at a family council, presided over by Uncle George, on the surest means to shave points off the income tax return. "It's O.K., Kid," his uncle said. "Everybody does it."

When he was nine, his mother took him to his first theater production. The box office man couldn't find any seats until his mother discovered an extra two dollars in her purse. "It's O.K., Son," she said. "Everybody does it."

When he was 12, he broke his glasses on the way to school. His Aunt Francine persuaded the insurance company that they had been stolen and they collected $27. "It's O.K., Kid," she said. "Everybody does it."

When he was 15, he made right guard on the high school football team. His coach showed him how to block and at the same time grab the opposing end by the shirt so the official couldn't see it. "It's O.K., Kid," the coach said. "Everybody does it."

When he was 16, he took his first summer job at the big market. His assignment was to put the over-ripe tomatoes in the bottom of the boxes and the good ones on top where they would show. "It's O.K., Kid," the manager said. "Everybody does it."

When he was 18, Johnny and a neighbor applied for a college scholarship. Johnny was a marginal student. His neighbor was in the upper three percent of his class, but he couldn't play right guard. Johnny got the assignment. "It's O.K.," they told him. "Everybody does it."

When he was 19, he was approached by an upper classman who offered the test answers for three dollars. "It's O.K.," they told him. "Everybody does it."

Johnny was caught and sent home in disgrace. "How could you do this to your mother and me?" his father said. "You never learned anything like this at home." His aunt and uncle also were shocked.

If there's one thing the adult world can't stand, it's a kid who cheats. . . .

Reprinted from the *Chicago Sun-Times*.

10/31/91

Dear Jack,

I guess I've told you many times that I was proud of you. Times you played well and were a good sport on the tennis courts, I told you. Times you achieved good grades, I told you.

But Jack, I have never been so proud of you as I was last night when you recounted your telling Henry, "Your values are just different than mine."

First, I was proud that *you have values*. Not everyone does, Jack. Not everyone really knows what is right and what is wrong. You will meet a lot of people in life who take the easy way, shade the truth, or cut the corners, and they really have no sense of *what* they are doing.

Jack, you *have* values. You don't lie. You don't steal. You don't look out for yourself first and to hell with everyone else. You don't cheat. You have always been taught to *Do what's right*. And you *know* what's right. Not everyone does. Not everyone cares.

Second, I was proud that *you stand up for your values*. It's so easy to go along, not make waves, be the same as everyone else, be "one of the guys," not be different. More people get in trouble when they are young by "going along" than for any other reason. More drugs get taken by kids that want to "be one of the guys" than for any other reason. Most kids start smoking because their friends are. Most kids get drunk to "go along with the crowd." Allan killed a friend when driving drunk. He told his parents he *had to* drink because all of his fraternity brothers were drinking and getting drunk. Swell.

The interesting thing is that your friends will respect you more when you do stand up for what you know to be right. They may not admit it but *they do*. That isn't to say you will always be the most popular. Sometimes the easygoing kid who just goes along is *very* popular . . . but respect, no!

So when you stand up for what you know is right, for your values, even with a roommate, I'm proud of you. You know you have to finish what you start. You know you have to play fair. You know you have to do your share of the chores. You know you don't leave a mess for the next guy to clean up. You know to be on time. You know that you don't get away with stuff just because you can. You know you don't waste things. You know you don't pick on smaller people. You know to keep your word. You know what good manners are. You know that you should respect people in positions of authority (even when they don't always earn that respect). . . . And Jack, it shows!!!

Maybe Henry will learn a bit from your example and be better for it.

Anyway, Jack . . . I'm proud of you.

Dad

Will the Real You Please Stand Up?

Submit to
pressure
from peers
and you move
down to their
level.
Speak up
for your own
beliefs
and you invite
them up to your
level.
If you move
with the crowd,
you'll get
no further than
the crowd.
When 40 million
people believe in
a dumb idea,
it's still a
dumb idea.
Simply swimming
with the tide
leaves you
nowhere.
So if you
believe in

something
that's good,
honest and bright—
stand up for it.
Maybe your peers
will get smart
and drift
your way.

© United Technologies
Corporation 1983 and reprinted
from the *Wall Street Journal*.

11/6/91

Dear Jack,

Let's talk about your life . . . specifically, *losing it.* Kids your age usually can't fathom death but *it happens.* As a matter of fact, young men die more frequently than middle-aged men. Only old men die with greater frequency than teenage men. So it's something to consider if you value your life (which you do) and don't want to die (which you don't).

So, what causes young men to die?

#1 *Booze.* . . . Just yesterday, on the news, a fraternity boy died of alcohol poisoning. He drank over 28 ounces of vodka at a party and he died in two days with brain damage and kidney failure. Mostly, though, boys end up with a death from drunk driving accidents (like Allan's friend). The problem is that drinking is almost a sport, taking the forbidden fruit, a rite of manhood, or "everybody is doing it" to a teenager. And most teenagers don't know their capacity for booze or how it will really affect them.

OK, you will drink, you already have. I did when I was a teenager. So how to do it and not die.

Rule A. . . . *Know how much beer or booze it takes for you to lose your power of reasoning well.* Usually that will be about 3 drinks or 3 or 4 beers. . . . At that point your judgment is shot. And it's when your judgment is shot that you think you can drive or go in a car with a drunk.

Rule B. . . . *Never drink to just get drunk.* That's just inviting disaster. It's no fun to be drunk, and it's no fun to wake up the next day feeling horrible. Kids that like to get drunk have a problem and need help.

Rule C. . . . When you find yourself in a situation (like a party) where you are under pressure to drink with everyone else . . . *count* what you drink and stay in control of yourself.

Social drinking (i.e., one or two drinks at a party or a couple of beers or wine with dinner) is OK. Out-of-control drinking is a recipe for suicide. Date rape situations, getting a girl pregnant, and 95% of auto fatalities happen when kids have had too much to drink. . . . So be careful, stay in control of yourself, and you'll stay alive.

#2 Accidents. . . . Kids just don't seem to understand the realities of danger.

Motorcycles are sure death . . . it's only a question of how long it will be before you hit the ground . . . and the ground is a lot harder than your head. The horror is to be permanently disfigured or become a lifelong cripple. . . . That's almost worse than being dead. It's just plain not worth the fun of riding a bike.

Stupid, risk-prone sports like rock climbing, hang gliding, etc., cause a lot of accidents. You just have to be careful and not engage in high-risk activities . . . the risk just isn't worth it . . . the downside just isn't worth the fun.

#3 Fights with strangers. . . . If some idiot flips you the bird or cuts you off when driving . . . *ignore it*. You don't have to be macho and come on tough. The idiot may have a knife or a gun. He may not have much to lose, but *you do*.

OK, sport, there it is. Play by the rules and you will

significantly increase your chance of living through your teenage years and having a long and prosperous life. I don't want to cut you out of any fun, I just want you to have a full life to have fun.

You have always had a lot of common sense. Use it in the years to come. In this game of life *one mistake can be fatal.*

I love you very much, Jack
Dad

11/13/91

Dear Jack,

Let's talk about grades:

You settled down to business at Carden and got straight A's, that got you into Computech. There was competition at Carden but 5th & 6th grade work wasn't above your ability (for sure!).

Then you went to Computech and settled down to business. *The competition wasn't tough!* The grading standards weren't the highest at Computech. In two years there you got just 2 B's. And that got you into Cate.

Now you're at Cate and *it's a whole new world*!! The courses are tough. The competition *is* tough. (No loafers at Cate!) And the grading standard is high. So, *you got your first C and the rest A's and B's. . . . YOU CAN DO BETTER!!!*

I think part of the problem is that you have been having too good a time at Cate and, in your own words, *you have not been doing your best.*

Part of the problem is also one of adjustment. You are *just now* beginning to really get adjusted to the *challenges, competition,* and *standards* of a first-rate high school. And this is why kids that make it through a good one also make it to good colleges and then make it successfully through their lives!!

So what should you do now:

First of all, realize that you're a kid & having fun is part of being a kid. But your future is on the line and you're at Cate for an education. And *one* (just one) measurement of your education is your grades. So you have to get your priorities straight and *do your best* on the things that really count. And one of the most important is *grades*.

Second, don't be discouraged. You can do better and you will. What you are now experiencing is part of growing up. The *winners prevail*, the losers get discouraged and fall by the wayside. And you're a *winner*.

Third, and most important, identify what you need to do and establish a plan to do it. That means meeting with your teachers and anyone else that is competent to advise you. Talk about the situation and determine *how* and *specifically what* you are falling short in. Then *set up a plan to do better*. Maybe that means better study habits. Maybe that means taking better notes in class. Maybe that means listening better in class and *showing off less*. Then set your goals *realistically*. Try to raise a grade point each quarter (if that's how you want to do it). So you'll be where you ought to be and where you want to be, by a *certain date*.

Jack, I love you and I believe in you. I know that some part of your performance you do for me and/or because of some pressure I may or may not put on you. But in this game and from now on you have to *do it for you*. (And for a wife and children that will benefit from your education.) (And for all the payoffs you will enjoy as you go through your life.)

Your efforts at Carden and Computech got you where you are. Aren't you glad you got it together then? Your place at Cate now was earned then, night by night of homework and day by day of *your* effort. You will look back in four years, from a top college, and know your determination in 1991 is what got you there!!

Good Luck, old boy. I believe in you.

Love

Dad

Remember how you felt the day you got the Cate and Thacher letters? That's what it's about!!!

1/4/92

Dear Jack,

Let's talk about time. . . . You're fifteen and at your age "time" is a *very* intangible substance. A teenager's perception of "time" is either "right now" or "in a long time." When you want something you *always* have to have it "*right now.*" Any delay is awful!

When you were five, a year was a third of your conscious life, an eternity almost. A year to me is 2% of my life. Time seems to go so slowly at your age. At my age the months race by.

At some times in your life, all the experiences are new and the time flies by. At other times of repetitious activities, time drags.

And time is often a function of point of view. The story is of the older man in the office who says triumphantly to the younger man, "Take it from me, I have 20 years of experience." The younger man says, "No, you have one year of experience twenty times over."

Let's try to get a perspective of time. Jack, time has a linear dimension *and* a qualitative dimension.

The "linear" dimension of "time" means that one unit of it comes *after* the unit before and before the next unit. Thus, the time line:

Mon	Tues	Wed	Thurs	Fri	Sat	Sun	or,
J	F	M	A	M	J	J	A	S	O	N	D	or
1992		1993		1994		1995		1996

The *qualitative* dimension of "time" is a matter of perception: If you are having a good time and/or are very busy, then time passes very quickly, in your perception. If you're bored and/or are having a "bad" time, then your perception is that time is passing very slowly. Thus, the guy in jail feels that the weeks just drag by and the person who hates his job watches the clock all day long and feels that the day will *never* end.

It's hard to believe that your first year at Cate is half over. It seems that it was just yesterday that we drove away from Waldby Street and you entered Cate. You sure have packed a lot of growing and learning and maturing into the last four months!! Time has passed so quickly. That little guy that showed up at his dad's door so few years ago has come so far.

So, roughly five months to go this school year: January and February, then most of March on vacation at home, then April and May, then home in early June.

There are some other aspects of "time" that are important: Wasted time. High-intensity time. Relaxation time. Irreplaceable time. You were a little boy only once and I'm glad I spent so much time, irreplaceable time, with you (i.e., the zoo, the rodeo, Anniston, etc.). I'm sad that Steph and Derek are growing up and I'm missing so much of their irreplaceable time.

Remember some of the high-intensity time you have spent (like taking your SAT)?

So here's the drill: eight weeks until spring break:

		Steph Birthday	Dad to Cate		Derek Birthday	LA Book Fair			Home
6	13	20	27	3	10	13	24	2	4
	January				February			March	
week	#1	#2	#3	#4	#5	#6	#7	#8	#9	#10

Exam week at Cate . . . New Hampshire Primary Election
2½ weeks till Steph turns eight
5½ weeks till Derek turns twelve
3 weeks until I see you (after exams)
2 weeks to exams

OK, old boy. Think about time and its dimensions and perspectives. *Make the very most you can of this next eight weeks.* Do them one week at a time, each week one day at a time.

1. Please read over your grades and the teachers' comments. . . . Take them to heart and keep them on your mind these next eight weeks.
2. Please read my letter about grades. There are some important thoughts there, if I do say so myself.

Jack, I love you and I'm with you all the way!!
Dad

1/5/92

Dear Jack,

Just a quick note to add to my letter of last night and get it in the mail.

Frazzle has lost it! She is on your bed crying and crying. Boy does she miss you. . . . So do I!!

I washed your shirt and it's in your room. I'll deposit the $50 to your account when the bank opens this morning.

I plan to see you January 25th (we can go out for dinner and take a friend if you like).

I'll be going to the book fair in LA and having Valentine's Day with Jan on February 14th and 15th. . . . If you would like to join us or if you would like me to stop by on the way home, I will . . . *or* I could bring Steph and Derek down to see you (we could go to Jan's in LA and do something special) on February 22nd and 23rd.

I'll pick you up March 4th and you will have almost three weeks at home. Let me know what you would like to do on your vacation. Would you like to take a trip, plan some skiing, whatever? You will have 3 days of drivers ed. and training. Then I'm *never* going to drive again.

Let me know your thoughts on the above. . . . I love you.

Dad

P.S. Thanks for the hat . . . I love it!

1/27/92

Dear Jack,

Enclosed are a couple of news clips. Some serious, some not. . . . Thought you might want to see them.

I'm glad your exams are over and I'll bet you are, too. . . . Too bad you were sick, that probably took your "edge" down, but that's life in the fast lane.

I'm still up in the air about your Easter vacation schedule. Would you write me about your desires?

1st: Wed., Mar. 4th . . . do you want me to pick you up (and Mark) or do you want to come home with Mark?

2nd: What days do you want to do drivers training?

3rd: You ought to spend a couple days with your mother, when? The kids will be there the 14th & 15th so maybe that would be a good time.

4th: What would you like to do, see, accomplish during your 2½ weeks at home? Any ideas?

This Saturday I'll bring the kids down to Thacher and we'll watch your game. That will be something since you could have been playing for Thacher. Then we'll have dinner with you, spend the night at the Miramar, and do whatever you want Sunday morning. We'll have to leave about 1:00 Sunday.

Love you, Son

Dad

2/13/92

Dear Jack,

Terry Eagle [Jack's counselor—ed.] may be pleased with your report card. *I'm not!*

After your last report we set some *realistic* goals *together* for what we could expect for the next period:

subject	1st quarter you got	you said you would try for		2nd quarter you actually got
Foundation Arts	B-	B+	<—goal—>	B+
English	B	A-		B
Topics	B+	A		B+
Spanish	B	A-		B
Chemistry/Bio	C+	B+	<—goal—>	B+
Math	B+	A		B+

You met your goal in two of six classes, ⅓!! You showed *no improvement* in four of six classes, ⅔!!

And look at the teachers' comments in the classes where you had *no improvement*:

English . . . "Too little, too late." "Jack needs to assess his current study habits." "He should start taking notes in class and focus." (You have heard "focus" before, huh?)

Topics . . . "I don't think he is pushing himself." "Jack should be a solid 'A' student and could be were he to work at it." (There is no greater sin, Jack . . . I'm crushed!!)

Arts . . . "Distracting in class." (Swell!)

Spanish . . . "If he were more focused [there's that word again] and diligent on daily assignments he could do better." "He needs to . . . sustain concentration and prepare more thoroughly."

Well, they have about said it all, haven't they? And what about your adviser's comment, "it will only come when Jack applies that pressure himself."

OK, Jack, when will that be? And what will it take to convince you that your future and all your dreams are riding on your success at Cate?

I suggested that you meet with your Spanish, English, and Topics teachers and ask them for help in getting on track. But you haven't bothered to do that, have you?

Jack, I'm quite disappointed, to say the least. Your improvement in two of your classes is sure indication that you *can* do it *when* and *where you want* to. If your teachers were telling me that you were busting your ass and just couldn't do better than C's, I would have no gripe. *"That ain't the case!!"*

Come down off your high horse. Quit the fooling around (you can still have fun and be popular).

The teachers say "focus." Well if you don't know what that means you better find out. They say "concentrate." You better get some help if you don't know how to "concentrate" already.

But mostly, it's the *effort*, focused, concentrated effort, that is needed. And as Mr. Eagle said, *"The pressure to do it has to come from you!!"*

You now have two weeks before your spring break. . . . Use the time wisely.

I have enclosed your report card with the grades I believe you *can* meet this quarter. I don't think I have been unrealistic.

Love

Dad

2/13/92

Dear Jack,

Received your most welcome letter this morning and I hasten to reply.

I've enclosed a worksheet for your spring break. . . . You can fill it in with what you would like to do, where you would like to go, etc., etc. I'm looking forward very much to your being home. I miss you a lot and the time we used to spend talking, kidding, going to the store, etc. Your spring break will be fun.

I'm really looking forward to your lacrosse game Saturday. I've *never* seen lacrosse played before. You said on the phone last night that the Thacher/Cate game for Wednesday was canceled. Does that mean you have two Thacher/Cate games to go, one of which will be played Saturday? If so, perhaps I can come down for the other one and see two. I sure as hell hope the rain misses Saturday's game. I really want to see it, particularly since you could have been playing for Thacher.

I liked your idea of a bit of an adventure in the mountains together while you're home. Maybe we could take a day hike out of Wawona. There are some really beautiful mountains just in back of the hotel.

By the way, would you like a subscription to *Surfer* magazine? I got a copy the other day at Wavelengths when I was there buying Derek's present. I thought I might learn a bit about the sport. It had a column on "creekspeak" (i.e., Barnold: Barney & Arnold = a kook).

The floods in Ventura County have been all over the news. (CNN was feeding direct a good part of the day.)

Here in Fresno we got an inch or so but nothing like the 8+ inches that parts of LA and Ventura County got.

I went in to see Steph's teacher yesterday. She is doing fine in school. Derek's report cards are still mostly B's. . . . He can do a lot better. I called Charlie and a friend of mine on the school board about Derek. I think he is going to make it into Computech.

Well, that's it for now. . . . See you Saturday.

Dad

P.S. I still haven't gotten the itemization of your lacrosse bill.

2/16/92

Dear Jack,

After World War I, Winston Churchill, paraphrasing the Duke of Wellington, said, "The victories on the battlefields of Europe were won on the playing fields of Eton." What he meant was that the leadership of England formulated its character, determination, perseverance, and teamwork as youngsters in the classrooms and on the playing fields of their best schools.

I never had a better sense of what Churchill meant than yesterday watching your lacrosse game with Thacher. On that field were some of the major business and community leaders of California in the years to come.

Some of the boys cut corners a bit when the referee wasn't looking, some showboated, some just went through the motions and never really put out their best effort, and some blew it each time the pressure was on them. Some were leaders and playmakers and some were not. I couldn't believe little Mark Albertson charging into a boy time after time who had him by 10 inches and forty pounds. And he never let up.

And I was very proud of my son. You were a leader, you had that undefinable quality called "presence." You never showed fear; you charged the ball time after time and mowed down whoever was in the way. You took the good shots and made the first score of the game. You set Mark up time after time (if he had made half of the shots you gave him, Cate would have had the game) and passed it off very well to your teammates. You stayed in the whole game and never quit. I was proud of you.

You got a bit discouraged and lightened up somewhat in the second half. I think you could have realized your mood and talked it up a bit for *yourself and your teammates*. Maybe you could have backed them up and the score would have been different. I've seen that in your tennis.

Jack, I can't believe what a great natural athlete you are. . . . You are truly gifted. . . . Make the most of that God-given talent, old boy.

I'm really glad I drove four hours to see you play and four hours home. It was more than worth it.

Jack, let's talk a moment about character and excellence, *mostly excellence*.

Character really isn't much more than "doing the right thing." How many times we've talked about that! Maybe some people don't really even *know* what the right thing is . . . it's hard for them to have "character." . . . You *do* know what the "right thing" is! God knows I've tried to show you and tell you and put you in places where you could see it for yourself.

And as your father, I could not be more pleased that, for the most part, you translate your knowledge of what is right into "doing what's right." And that, old boy, is character. And you have it.

Now, what about excellence? Every man's quest for excellence is part of his character (or lack of character). It's harder for some than others. . . . Some are gifted in some areas and some are not. (Look at Mark on the playing field . . . he isn't gifted . . . his effort and courage takes real character!!)

I know that in my life some things have come easy and some have really taken hard work and determination. Doing the right thing has not always been easy, and sometimes I've failed. Sometimes I haven't really shown "character." In some areas I did not really try to achieve the excellence I was capable of.

I think that's what your Topics teacher is talking about when he says, "Jack needs to focus on the development of his ideas . . . much of what he writes is rather superficial. . . . Jack should be a solid 'A' student if he were to work at it." Now, Jack, I know you. And I know your Topics teacher isn't really your cup of tea (he isn't mine either). You don't have the "chemistry" with him that you have with your math teacher. So you're not really pushing yourself in his class. You're not really pushing yourself for him.

Wrong!!

1. It's *for yourself*, not for him. It's *you* that will have to live with what you've learned from him and the grade you got . . . not him.
2. Whether you hit it off with him or not, he has much to offer you. You don't only learn from those you like. You cannot let whether you "click" with a teacher dictate how much you put into a class (or don't put into it). And that, my son, takes *character*. And that's what gripes your English teacher, too.

3. Playing little "one-up" games with a teacher you don't appreciate takes no character. You beat him by seeking excellence *in spite* of him.

So, my son, I love you and I'm with you all the way. You know that. *Seek Excellence!!* Strengthen your character with the same pride that you strengthen your body. Put out the effort even where it isn't easy. Learn from those you don't really hit it off with. . . . Beat them with your determination to be *excellent* in spite of them . . . then *you* win.

I love you, Jack

Dad

4/7/92

Dear Jack,

I want to let you know how much I appreciate your most welcome call tonight. Not only could I hear you for a change (which took some effort on your part to walk down-and-up the hill) but the news was great:

QUARTERS	1	2	3	POTENTIAL FINAL
Foundation Arts	B-	B+	B-	B+
English	B	B	(B+)	(A-)
Topics	B+	B+	B+	(A-)
Spanish	B	B	(B+)	(A-)
Chemistry/Bio	C+	B+	(A)	A
Math	B+	B+	(A)	A

Note the improvements circled.

Note your potential 4th quarter which *ought to be your final grade*. As far as I'm concerned that's a straight A.

Jack, I could not be more pleased!! What a wonderful way to welcome your dad to Parents' Weekend!! How proud I am of you. You've been working and it shows!!

Jack, you are so close to a great college you ought to be able to taste it. You have a month and a half to bear down and you'll be a "straight A" student. You can't get much better, and boy will you see how worth it it will be . . . for all your life.

Thank you, Jack . . . you're really doing it.

Love

Dad

4/22/92

Dear Jack,

Another short note with a couple of articles you will want to read.

I'm thinking of you. I didn't hear from you again over the weekend so I assume you had a good time, got your homework done, and made it back to school OK.

Yesterday was quite a day in Fresno. It was the 50th anniversary of the Doolittle raid on Tokyo. (Remember the movie *30 Seconds over Tokyo?*) Five B-24s took off from a carrier in San Diego, flew to Monterey where they dropped a ton of flowers over Doolittle's home (he is 95), and then flew into Fresno with an escort of four P-51s. They did 3 fly-bys over the airport and then landed. It was very dramatic and moving. I wish you had been there. . . . It was great! What an honor for a true American hero. . . .

Enclosed are four stamps. Can I expect a couple letters from you?

Good luck on your studies. Work hard, old boy, it will be worth it! I promise! Focus, pay attention, pace yourself, and concentrate. . . . I'm sure you will do that.

Love

Dad

EXCUSES, EXCUSES
BY THOMAS SOWELL

"The worst continued to worsen," John Kenneth Galbraith said, in his entertaining account of the stock market crash of 1929. Unfortunately, that also applies to American education today.

Recently released statistics show that American high school students have now reached an alltime low in their verbal scores on the Scholastic Aptitude Test, taken by more than a million young people preparing to go on to college. Looking back over the past 30 years, the highest SAT scores were reached in 1963, the entire decade of the 1970s saw declines every year, and the minor improvements of the 1980s never reached the levels achieved 20 years earlier.

Now the 1990s have begun with a new decline to a record low. The worst continues to worsen.

With years of experience in dealing with bad results, the educational establishment has become expert at explaining them away. The first line of defense is that the results don't mean anything. A favorite variation is that American colleges are now providing "access" to so many "disadvantaged" students that of course the average scores of those applying to college are a little lower.

Unfortunately for this argument, test scores have been declining *at the top*. Twenty years ago, more than 116,000 students scored above 600 on the SAT (out of a possible 800). Today, with slightly more students taking the test, fewer than 75,000 score that high. In math, about the same proportion score above 600 as in 1971. However, we must remember that 1971 was not a golden age. The decline was already under way for several years by then.

When declining results on a wide variety of tests cannot be talked away, educators then argue that this shows a need for more money to be spent on the public schools. Thus the tables are turned and "society" is put on the moral defensive for having "neglected" the education of the next generation by not "investing" enough in their education, condemning them to "overcrowded classrooms" and the like.

In reality, the U.S. spends more money per pupil than most other nations, including nations whose youngsters consistently outperform ours on international tests. We spend more money than Japan, for example, whether measured in real per-pupil expenditures or as a percentage of our gross national product. We have fewer pupils per class than Japan, and in mathematics our classes are less than half the size of Japanese math classes. The only thing we don't have are results. American students have come in last in international math tests.

"Society" has not failed its children. The public schools have failed. That is what all the clever evasions and distractions seek to conceal.

There is really nothing very mysterious about why our public schools are failures. When you select the poorest-quality college students to be public school teachers, give them iron-clad tenure, a captive audience, and pay them according to seniority rather than performance, why should the results be surprising?

Money is not the problem here, either. Better-qualified people become private school teachers at lower salaries. The crucial problem is with the filter through which the overwhelming majority of teachers pass—education courses. Mediocrity and incompetence pass readily through such filters, but education courses repel the more able and intelligent college students. Paying higher salaries to the kind of people who emerge from this process only makes mediocrity and incompetence more expensive.

It is not simply the dullness or the shallowness of education courses that is crucial, nor it is simply the academic deficiencies of the people who choose to take these courses. Rather, it is the fatal attraction of *nonacademic* projects to people for whom academics have never been a source of achievement or pride. Throughout this century, there has been an ongoing struggle between laymen trying to focus the public schools on teaching academic subjects, while the educators have increasingly gone off into the wild blue yonder of endless nonacademic fads.

While students in Japan are studying math, science and a foreign language, American students are sitting around in circles unburdening their psyches (and family secrets) in a wide range of psycho-babble courses called "affective education." What with "nuclear education," multiculturalism, environmentalism and a thousand other world-saving crusades, our students are learning to "express themselves" on all sorts of issues for which neither they nor their teachers have even the rudiments of competence.

It is going to be difficult to get teachers who are even

academically oriented, much less academically able, as long as education courses are the legally mandated filter through which the vast majority of teachers pass. Such courses are legal prerequisites solely because of the political muscle of the education establishment, whose top priority is preserving the jobs of its own. Forty million American school children are thus sacrificed to preserve the jobs of fewer than 40,000 professors of education. That's more than a thousand youngsters sacrificed for every education professor.

Reprinted from *Forbes*.

SPARE THE PROD,
SPOIL THE CHILD
BY DYAN MACHAN

Does learning how to cope with pressure at an early age necessarily put you on the track to being a better manager or scientist?

Educators at the privately funded Johns Hopkins Center for Talented Youth think so. Their thesis is that the best students often go unchallenged in the classroom, can't move at their own pace and are ultimately frustrated and turned off by the educational process. Their solution: Push kids as hard as you can, as early as you can.

Underchallenging the best and brightest, they argue, will shortchange this country of future leaders. Lighting fires under the talented is at least as important as providing remedial programs for the less gifted, and probably more so. Along with recently publicized falling test scores among high school students, William Durden, the Johns Hopkins Center director, cites two other grim facts: Japan has passed the U.S. in the number of patents per year, and, according to the International Association for the Evaluation of Educational Achievement, top U.S. students rank at the bottom in math and science among developed nations.

On the other side are those who say programs for the gifted are elitist and needlessly stressful to impressionable young minds. And to save money, Connecticut, New York and California are cutting back on these programs.

John Katzman, founder of Princeton Review, a firm that prepares kids to take aptitude tests, says some gifted programs are great. But he warns parents: "It's not worth making your kids crazy about."

The Hopkins program is one of the largest and oldest of more than 35 centers nationwide that offer gifted kids from ages 11 to 17 a chance to take advanced courses during summer and after school. How do you define "gifted"? Even the 11-year-olds in the program must have at least 930 out of a possible 1600 combined math and verbal score on the Scholastic Aptitude Test. The national average is 896 for college-bound seniors.

"Stress is not a dirty word," says Durden. "Stress and competition are important for educational advancement. The American school system has gone out of its way to eliminate every form of academic competition. Some schools shy away from using standardized tests for their brightest students for fear the comparison may harm the students' self-esteem."

How tough is the Johns Hopkins program? A FORBES reporter visited a program run by the Johns Hopkins Center on the Skidmore College campus—one of six colleges where CTY offers classes. This summer over 500 students attended the Skidmore three-week summer sessions, where they took high school- and college-level courses in subjects like math, history and writing.

At Skidmore, the first thing one notices is that boys and girls are about evenly divided, with a heavy representation of Asian teenagers but few blacks or Hispanics.

Second, these kids, apart from their intelligence, are otherwise normal. So normal that many seem a bit embarrassed to be there; they are often unwilling to tell their friends back home they attend "nerd camp." Matthew Keeler, 16, a sophomore at Ridgefield High School, in Ridgefield, Conn., says his friends just wouldn't understand the appeal of spending five hours a day in classroom lectures and at least two more hours each evening studying under strict supervision.

Keeler, who concedes his parents bribed him with a new leather jacket to take the Scholastic Aptitude Test at 13 instead of the normal 17, has attended the courses for the last three summers. Despite his slight embarrassment at being there, he's unquestionably happy he is: "Here you can have an intelligent conversation."

Stress? It's there. Take Jennifer Nam, a quiet, rule-abiding 15-year-old. The school's rule is that students' lights are out at 10:15 P.M., but Nam, a sophomore at Watchung Hills Regional High School in New Jersey, breaks the rule. Enrolled in European history, Nam, whose parents came from Korea, says, "I was so lost. Everyone knows what's going on but me." To keep up, she sometimes got up at 5:30 A.M. and stayed up to 11:30 P.M. So how does the overworked, overwhelmed Nam feel about the demanding program? "I love it."

She's not alone in having to stay on her toes. Here 11-to-17-year-olds take a full year of high school chemistry, for instance, in 15 days.

Yes, there's plenty of stress. In some classes, competition means self-esteem is actively bashed. In a writing course, for example, eight students and a teacher form a semicircle around a 14-year-old who looks as if she's ready to cry. Her classmates have each read her essay, and each gets a crack at ripping it apart. The final blow comes from the teacher, Philip Boshoff: "Your observations are insightful, but your writing sounds stupid." The 14-year-old bites her lip, looks down but doesn't cry.

Boshoff explains why he was so tough on the girl: These students are so accustomed to getting A's and pats on the back for everything they turn in that they no longer feel challenged in regular schools. "They generally thank me for the constructive criticism they never had," Boshoff says.

Connie Chuang, 15, a sophomore at Dwight Englewood, in Englewood, N.J., says she wishes she could study math all day long. What she hated was having to break for the activities like volleyball or choir. Says Chuang, "Math is awesome."

What many of the students seem to dread most is going back to their regular high schools, where they'll probably be intellectually undernourished. Says Keeler: "That's like giving a weight lifter 10-pound weights to work out."

These kids are saying something important: Spare the prod, spoil the child.

Reprinted from *Forbes*

4/24/92

Dear Jack,

I really appreciated your call last evening. It's a pleasure to be able to talk to you on a clear phone and where you can really talk.

You might want to look at the summer schedule again. It ought to be self-explanatory. It shows where we have things scheduled and *thus* where you are free to fill in (hopefully from the options I listed . . . and not just lay around). There are 14 weeks in the summer. It ought to be a great summer for you!

Work hard on your studies. . . . *It will be worth it!!* . . . Only three weeks until exams. . . . Only four weeks until you are home. I'm really looking forward to spending time with you this summer.

See you this weekend.

     Love

        Dad

P.S. Write a note to Barsotti!!

SOPHOMORE
YEAR

9/24/92

Dear Jack,

It was good to see you Wednesday afternoon. . . . Sorry you weren't playing. The cocktail party was sort of fun. The parents were an interesting and diverse group, from old hippies to business and academic types.

I was very impressed with Beth. She was quite poised . . . as are you . . . and a very beautiful young lady. Jan was also impressed (and coming from a woman, that's important!). I enjoyed your *nonflamboyant* hand holding and *mild* gestures of affection. . . . They seemed genuine and in good taste and not overdone. Obviously, she cares for you and isn't ashamed to show it. . . . Great!! Jan's comment was, "Well, he's off the market for the next three years." I wouldn't go that far, but it could be a lot worse than that. Treat her well, be thoughtful, *communicate* with her, and be sensitive. I'm sure you will be all of that. Don't rush things!!! And don't get so wrapped up with her that you forget why you're at Cate . . . and that's not for women. I remember a ten-year-old boy telling me, "'Going around' makes life more fun!" . . . when he was "going around" with a girl named Justine. Anyway, you done good, ol' boy . . . good luck. Steph called yesterday, and said she was going to write you a letter. Derek has the flu, and is home.

I'm planning to come down Wednesday the 7th for your birthday. We might want to take Beth out to dinner. If that sounds good, let me know. If that's what you would like, I'll clear it with the school.

Next week (I hope this will reach you before you leave for Yosemite but if not, I'll tell you when you call), Dan will give you and Beth a room (separately of course) to shower. . . . Call him if you need anything and you should *stop by to see him* and see Grayson while you're in the park.

Now then, your math class. Jack, *when you have a problem, you need to let me know*. The drawback of your being away at school is that I'm out of touch unless *you keep me informed!! Quick!!* Now then, that being said, let's get a tutor for your math before you fall behind and can't catch up. You might remember though, with math, that sometimes you can go a couple of weeks thinking it's all a fog and then, ZAP, it all of a sudden becomes clear. Let's stay with it, work hard, ask your teacher for some extra explanations, or maybe even a junior or senior that's a math whiz. But the main thing is not to stay in a fog without help and fall more and more behind. . . . Good Luck, Jack!!!

I've enclosed a couple of articles for you to read. Note the one on the dead teenager: (1) On the freeway or a main road between 10:00 P.M. and 2:00 A.M. (2) No safety belt. (3) A right front seat death. And (4) an inexperienced driver who lost control in an emergency.

I enclosed the preliminary SAT (one for you and one for Beth). . . . Invest 17 minutes of your time to take it. . . . Let me know the results.

Well, old boy, that's about it for now. I'm happy with how hard you're working. I'm proud of your choice in women. I'm proud of your poise and the way you're growing up.

Keep up the good work.

       Love

           Dad

I've enclosed some stamps. . . . I'd like to get a letter or two, too!!!

P.S. Since it's Friday and you couldn't get this before you leave, I'll send this to Dan and ask him to see that you get it.

           Dad

10/7/92

Dear Jack,

Happy 16th Birthday!!!

This is a very special day; not only is it your birthday, Jack, but it's your 16th birthday! It's a day in your life that you will never forget; where you are, who you're with and where you spent your birthday dinner, and what you got for your birthday. It's more than just a birthday, *it's a rite of passage*. It's almost like being grown up . . . *almost*! By God, you can drive now!! . . . by yourself . . . and that means you can come and go *as* you please, *when* you please, *where* you please. And the State of California will license you to do so (if your parents say so and *I do say so*). You've earned my trust in a million ways and never violated the trust you have earned. So it's yours and I have no second thoughts.

So now you're 16!! The oldest aphorism is "Sweet sixteen and never been kissed." Well, Jack, so much for that one!! But you *have* retained an innocence about you that is wonderful. Jack, never lose that 16-year-old innocence, and your idealism and enthusiasm for life's experiences . . . even if you're 46! Some kids burn out so early and never have what you have. You're lucky.

Let's take a moment to benchmark where you *really* are: *16* . . . that's 5,840 days, 140,160 hours, or 8,409,600 minutes of life. You've lived in three houses and one school away from home. You've gone through eleven grades of school in three *different* schools plus a preschool. You've traveled to twelve states plus the District of Columbia and one foreign country. You've been in 50 of California's 58 counties. You've met the President, Senators and Congressmen, Generals and heads of Corporations. You've climbed mountains and dived in the ocean. You play tennis, ski, swim, ride, golf (acceptably), play soccer and lacrosse well, and are learning your second language. You have your health and are beginning to be fairly well-informed about the world. You have many friends, some important, some not so important. And you have left a strong impression wherever you have been, from Small World [preschool—ed.] to Carden to Computech to Cate. And the impression has been positive! I will never forget Mrs. Nebeker saying, "and Jack . . . well, he's *Jack*!" You were different, special, someone to be remembered.

I take some pride, as your father, in the contribution I have made to your life. But, in a very real sense, *you have made yourself what you will be from now on*!!

I have so enjoyed each year of your life and watching you become a man. And each day, each talk together, each trip, each experience has enriched my life and upped the ante of each breath I take. I treasure them. The threads that weave through your life, like the little boy of three that didn't like "fighters," who became the young man who called his dad to kill a spider in his bathroom, have become the tapestry of *my son*. I am so proud of him.

You are my son, my friend, my severest critic and a wonderful companion. You have come so far and done so much and accomplished so much. Happy Sixteenth birthday Jack, and in the real spirit of the phrase: Many More to Come!!

    Love

        Dad

10/8/92

Dear Jack,

Just spoke to you and I called Truscott and OK'd your weekend.

Jack, I had a great time with you and Beth last night. One mission, along with sharing your birthday, was to let Beth get to know you a bit better and to get to know me (and thus you) a bit. . . . Mission accomplished!

Youngsters have a bit of a problem with "*roles*": son/father, teacher/student, customer/waiter, doctor/patient, etc. Last night's little object lesson *made a point*. I suspect you won't forget it, though, at the time, it offended your tender sensitivities.

You asked if you could share my letters with Beth. . . . I appreciated your loyalty and sense of discretion in asking. The answer is, "sure." If there is anything you shouldn't show Beth, I'll point it out.

Jack, I am *very* impressed with Beth. She is bright, direct, not a game player, beautiful, affectionate, and fun. Next time we get together, I'd like to really get to know *her* better. Oh yes, I could add, poised, tolerant, well mannered, great legs, etc., etc. Anyway, I think you have great taste in women and I thoroughly approve . . . and if I didn't . . .

Next Sunday, Tuesday, and Thursday evenings are the presidential debates. I want you to *make sure* you watch them. And I will look forward to hearing your comments.

I spoke with Jim Lake today and he thinks the president will be able to pull it out. They have some real bombshells to drop on Clinton . . . The sooner the better, I say!! Lake and I both agree that Clinton is one of the most unprincipled politicians to hit the national scene in as long as we can remember. The man will literally say anything or do anything to get in office and he stands for nothing but *power*, his power and the power of government (i.e., the bureaucrats) over the lives of the productive citizens of America.

Two weeks from now is "Parents' Weekend." I've made reservations at the Miramar for Friday and Saturday night. I'm not sure what the schedule is but I suspect I'll get to Cate early Friday and attend classes with you and then go through the prescribed activities Friday and Saturday. I don't plan to stay Sunday. I hope that either Friday evening or Saturday evening we will be able to have dinner with Beth's mother and father (I promise I won't embarrass you). Whatever the other evening is, you can figure we'll do whatever you like, and/or have dinner with whoever, or wherever you like.

Oh yes, I forgot, I'll send Beth a couple of photos of you. They will be good ones so don't worry.

Love

Dad

10/21/92

Dear Jack,

Enclosed is perhaps the saddest article I have ever read. . . . *Please read it!!*

Bottom line is that Papagni got in trouble financially and he *stole money* to try to get out of trouble (the old saying: "Desperate men do desperate things"). And he got caught! Do you think for *one moment* he would be delivering an "emotional apology" if he hadn't been caught?

I've seen it many times before, the worst cases being Gauvin, Bartman, and Yang. My business has been turning around troubled companies, so I've seen the temptations and the men who fell to them. I've also seen men under pressure who *did not* do dishonorable things to save their ass!

The thing that makes this so sad is that Papagni dragged his son down with him, and his son *let* him!

Jack, in the real world, things are seldom straightforward, black or white. And there is always an excuse. I'm sure Papagni figured that the "greater good" was saving his family business. There is always a reason (read: "rationalization"). Bartman was trying to "save" his other investors by "borrowing" from his trust accounts. He did and couldn't pay them back before they found out.

Jack, I've always said, "Do what is right." The analogue is: *"Don't do what's wrong."* That means breaking the rules (in letter or spirit), lying, cheating, stealing etc., etc. That means: Be honest, be truthful, be kind, be generous, be thoughtful, etc., etc.

The problem is, in real life, that it usually sneaks up on you. First, just a little shaving of the issue, and then it builds up. Bartman "borrowed" $25,000 for a week and paid it back. It was easy, so he "borrowed" $50,000 for a week, couldn't pay it back for two weeks, but he did pay it back. After a year or so he was in over a *million and a half* and *couldn't pay it back*. I'm sure Papagni started with just one load and if he had been caught, it would have been "a mistake." He didn't get caught so he did it again. Pretty soon he had falsified $1.8 million in shipments.

Can you imagine Papagni involving his son in the theft!!?? Can you imagine his son not saying, "Dad, *this is wrong.*" He says, "I love my father and I always will." . . . That's *not* the issue. He says, "I believe in him and I follow his advice." . . . Great!! He says, "It was wrong what I did." . . . No shit, Sherlock!! At least he accepted responsibility.

Anyway, like I said, that was the saddest article I've ever read. That Papagni did it was bad, but his getting his son involved was worse! The picture of a father *and* son in a federal criminal court being sentenced for a felony . . . God!!

You can bet Papagni never told his son, "Do what's right!" If he had and *if* his son had listened, perhaps it all would have been different. Perhaps the son could have saved his father.

Jack, I love you and I respect you. You have good

sense and you have good values. Use your good sense and keep your good values and you will have a great life.
    Love
                Dad

WINEMAKERS SENTENCED FOR SWITCH
BY ALEX PULASKI

Tearfully and humbly admitting that he cheated, Madera winemaker Angelo Papagni got the bill for it Monday: 18 months in federal prison.

Papagni and his son, Demetrio, were sentenced in federal court in Fresno for switching inexpensive barbera grapes for zinfandel grapes from 1985 to 1989. The two had pleaded guilty to misrepresenting the variety in selling 495,000 gallons of wine to such well-known wineries as Sutter Home and Glen Ellen.

Judge Oliver Wanger sentenced Demetrio Papagni, 33, to serve six months in a privately run halfway house in Fresno and pay a $10,000 fine. Demetrio Papagni will be allowed to remain free during work hours and serve time on nights and weekends.

In addition to the prison sentence, Wanger ordered Angelo Papagni, 71, to pay a $25,000 fine.

Both sentences were the lowest Wanger could order under federal sentencing guidelines without finding exceptional circumstances. The maximum term was five years.

The younger Papagni is scheduled to begin his sentence in December. The elder Papagni will be allowed to remain free until Demetrio is released next June. The elder Papagni had told Wanger before sentencing that a prison sentence would add nothing to the humiliation he had already suffered.

"I don't know how I can live it down after this," Angelo Papagni said. He said he had tarnished the reputations of his parents and other family members. He said he had blasted his son's future.

"I never in my life thought I would be in this position," Angelo Papagni said. "I thought I was beyond breaking the law."

The elder Papagni said he had been caught by financial pressures. Heavy debts and slow sales forced his winery into bankruptcy in 1988, and he saw that by selling his cheaper barbera grapes as zinfandel grapes he could realize a price that was $800 a ton higher.

"The only reason I did it is because I was up against the wall," he said.

More than two hours of the sentencing hearing was consumed by the Papagnis' attorneys, who attempted to show that the damages caused by misrepresenting the grape varieties were far lower than the government's estimate of $1.8 million.

Based upon Angelo Papagni's estimate, he made $396,000 during the four years that he could not have made by selling barbera grapes honestly. The difference in the two figures was significant because federal sentencing guidelines require longer terms for greater monetary damage.

Wanger accepted the lower figure.

Assistant U.S. Attorney R. Steven Lapham said the ultimate losers in the case were consumers, who paid premium prices for popular white zinfandel wines that had been watered down with a cheap variety. He said the reputation of the California wine industry had also been damaged.

Like his father, Demetrio Papagni delivered an emotional apology to the judge. His sentence was much lighter because his involvement was limited to switching documentation on the grapes during one year, 1988.

Attorneys said Demetrio Papagni took part in the scheme at his father's direction.

"I love my father and I always will," the younger Papagni said. "I believe in him and I follow his advice, although it was wrong what I did."

Reprinted from the *Fresno Bee*.

10/22/92

Dear Jack,

Several years ago you said you were too young to have sex and I agreed with your judgment. We agreed that we'd talk about it again when you were sixteen, but until then you'd keep your pants zipped. . . . *Now you're sixteen.*

There is a lot to consider when you're in a situation where "going all the way" is a possibility (or maybe even a *probability*).

First of all, let's use the term "make love" rather than "have sex." "Having sex" implies a purely physical act not unlike going to the toilet . . . relieving a physical urge.

In these days of rampant disease, getting involved with the kind of girl who will give "casual sex" is almost suicidal!! So let's confine this discussion to "making love," namely having a *total* physical relationship with a person you have a loving, caring, and monogamous relationship with.

Second, let's talk about the "down" sides before talking about morality or the "up" sides . . . not in order of importance necessarily:

Pregnancy. . . . A woman ovulates in the middle of her cycle and if she is "regular" that means her 14th day. Sperm live 24 hours, the egg 48 hours. So theoretically she gets pregnant if you make love on her 13th to 16th day. *But* young women are seldom "regular," so relying on counting days (the rhythm method) is a fairly sure way to be a father. You *do* decrease the risk if you limit making love to a couple of days after her period and a couple of days before *along with* some methods of birth control.

Everybody talks about condoms. Well, they are *better than nothing* but sometimes break, feel awful (in my opinion), and certainly break the mood when you have to put one on. But if that's all there is, *use one.* Birth control pills are much better but they too are *not fool-proof.* And some women don't want to use the pill or are embarrassed to ask their doctor for them. There are other methods (i.e., IUD, etc.) that we can talk about if you want.

Kids are great, you're my kid, but an unwanted kid fathered by a teenager is awful . . . for *the kid, the father,* and *the mother.* If you care enough for a girl to be with her, you ought to care enough for her *not to get her pregnant.*

Disease. . . . Let's look at reality: Herpes is *permanent,* there is no cure and it's a bitch! There are a *dozen* other sexually transmitted diseases that you can get that *can* be cured, but they are no fun either.

The key here, again, is *know your partner.* Their background, their habits, and what kind of person they are (she is).

Normal hygiene, use of a condom and staying with *one partner* will cut your odds to virtually "0," zip, zilch, nada.

Now then, the clinical stuff being passed, there is the *emotional:*

Unless you are a loose person, with no upbringing, then making love is a *high impact* thing. It profoundly changes a relationship! It adds a dimension to your life, personally, and hers. If it is your first experience, then *triple the stakes*. You will view her differently and yourself differently. For sure!!

Some men cannot help but lose respect for a girl they have made love to. . . . So much of society's teaching that "good girls don't" and "bad girls do" can't help but have an impact. That is changing but it's still a factor. Guard against this! And be aware of the reverse on the girl's part: guilt and insecurity. If you do, or *when* you do, be sensitive to her feelings afterward.

Some men cannot resist the urge to tell their friends or at least hint. *Don't!!* It's not fair to the girl, particularly in a small town or close community. And it makes the man seem like an insecure jerk! *Gentlemen don't talk!*

There is also that monthly anxiety. Worrying each month whether she is pregnant can, and will, put great pressure on a man and a relationship.

Oh yes, booze. . . . Drinking will reduce your (and her) inhibitions and self-control. In some ways, in moderation, that may be OK, but two half-swacked teenagers in love are a recipe for trouble!! So *realize the effects of booze.*

OK, the upside: the sharing of intimacy, being inside a woman and her having you inside her, the emotional force to bring a close couple even closer. It binds a couple and, in the case of teenage love, the shared "secret" makes an "us-against-the-world" situation.

But understand that the girl is the big "giver." It really shouldn't be seen that way but it is. So be sensitive to this fact. The girl is "seen" as more at risk, for her reputation *and* pregnancy!!

I've dwelled a lot on the downside and only a bit on the upside. And I haven't talked at all about morality. Morality is your own sense of values. I personally don't buy into the "it's bad" *period* position taken by most religious people. I don't buy into the guilt trips and "scarlet woman" and "only bad girls do" position. I also don't buy the "it's all OK" theory of free love. When you're older and more experienced perhaps the standards change a bit, but for teenagers, sex is *damn serious business*.

So, son, think the situation through well and, for sure, talk it out in detail with the lady involved, *before* you find yourself in the situation on the "sperm of the moment," so to speak (ha ha). I have a great deal of trust in your judgment and sense of what is right and wrong.

I've shared some, not all, of my wisdom on the topic. If you want to talk about it more, we can.

      Love

        Dad

10/23/92

Dear Jack,

I have tried very hard to *be* a good father (and you have made the job easy and a joy). Perhaps my effort was stimulated by the fact that I *did not have* a good father. That was a very important part of my life that I missed. And I see the effects of that lack every day of my life. I didn't want *my* son to miss a good relationship with a loving father.

One area that I failed you was that I divorced your mother. I can tell you that I could not stay married to her any longer. . . . I was *miserable.* And I can tell you that, other than the effect of my decision on you, Steph, and Derek, I have *never regretted it* . . . even during the *long, painful* divorce proceedings.

And, as I have compensated in later years for my early years, I'm sure you will too. You will be very *scared* of going through a divorce. So enclosed is probably the best article I have ever seen on predicting divorce. I think you will want to read the article many times over the years.

Love

Dad

TO PREDICT DIVORCE, ASK 125 QUESTIONS
BY JANE BRODY

With perhaps one in two marriages now ending in divorce, the toss of a coin might predict with 50 percent accuracy which marriages will survive.

Can science improve the odds of an accurate prediction, even to nearly 100 percent? Yes, say psychologists at the University of Washington in Seattle. They have devised an uncomplicated method that they contend will predict 94 times out of 100 which couples will still be married four years later.

Even among newlyweds, the psychologists say, the hallmarks of trouble can be readily determined years before a marriage dissolves.

The researchers, who have published their findings in the inaugural issue of the Journal of Family Psychology, said they were surprised to find that the husband's disappointment with the marriage was the single most potent predictor of divorce. Marital lore has long held that the wife is the best barometer of the health of a marriage.

The new study, directed by Dr. John Gottman, is one of a series of long-term investigations by him and collaborators into the factors that predict the length of marriage and divorce among couples of varying ages and circumstances. Most of the research is supported by grants from the National Institute of Mental Health.

Dr. David Olson, a family psychologist at the University

of Minnesota, said Gottman's findings were "very valuable and interesting" and agreed in principle with his own findings on hundreds of couples whom he has tested before marriage.

Olson devised a 125-item questionnaire used by about 20,000 clergymen and counselors nationwide to assess a couple's chances for a successful marriage.

"Our instrument, called Prepare, predicts with an accuracy of 80 to 85 percent which couples will divorce," he said.

Olson, who is director of the university's Marriage and Family Therapy Program, said many clergymen now insist on such premarital screening, and counseling when needed, before they will agree to marry a couple.

Dr. Susan Heitler, a Denver psychologist who studies the role of conflict in determining the length of marriages, said the kind of accuracy being reported by Gottman in predicting divorce suggests that "he is onto something intriguing and important."

Heitler has found that the intensity of the issues that cause conflict in a marriage and the skill with which couples try to deal with these issues are major predictors of marital unhappiness and dissolution.

Frequent arguing does not mean a couple is headed for the divorce court, Gottman and his collaborators found in a related study of long-lasting marriages.

"There can be a lot of arguing in a marriage that can also be marked by romanticism and affection," he said. "Whether they welcome conflict or avoid it, in couples that stay together, there are about five times more positive things said to and about one another than negative ones. But in couples that divorce, there are about 1½ times more negative things said than positive ones."

Gottman, who is also the author of "What Predicts Divorce," said the main tool used in his new study—an oral history questionnaire—could be applied by counselors to help couples recognize threats to their marriage.

Furthermore, Gottman and his co-authors, Kim Buehlman and Lynn Katz, say the questionnaire could become a computer test, allowing couples themselves to see if prenuptial counseling might improve their chances for a happy marriage.

According to the Seattle team, the assessment is the first of its kind to be applied to ostensibly happy young married couples. The 56 couples, all with a child ages 4 or 5, had on average a slightly higher than normal level of marital satisfaction when the study began in 1983.

Predictions Came True

The researchers found that among the 53 they were able to contact four years later, seven couples had divorced.

In their report, the researchers said they had predicted all seven of the divorces. They did, however, err in their prediction of the couples that would stay together. Three couples that the team believed would divorce were in fact still married four years later.

Still, the researchers said, their predictive success of

93.6 percent far exceeds any other method of detecting troubled marriages before the couples themselves are ready to call it quits.

The oral history interview, which was administered in the couples' homes, asked the husband and wife how they met, courted and decided to marry; their philosophy of what makes a marriage work, and how their marriage had changed over the years.

The researchers were less interested in the actual answers to the questions than in how the couple expressed themselves.

The couples were also observed in a "laboratory" setting during a 15-minute discussion of two problem areas in their marriages.

The psychologists then evaluated the results of the questionnaire and the discussion, looking at factors that in the past have been linked to relationships that run aground.

Though a "failing grade" on any one dimension may not doom a marriage, poor scores in several areas were associated with strains. These are the dimensions assessed:

- Affection toward the spouse.
- Negativity toward the spouse, which included vagueness about what attracted them to their spouse and how much they disagreed, and the negative feelings they expressed about each other.
- Expansiveness, or how expressive each partner was during the interview in, for example, giving details of the courtship.

• "We-ness" vs. separateness, or how much the spouses saw themselves as part of a team as opposed to emphasizing their independence.

• Gender stereotypes, or how much like "traditional" men and women the spouses were in their emotional expressions and responses and their roles in the family.

• Volatility, or intensity of their feelings toward each other when dealing with conflict.

• Chaos, a couple's feeling that they had little control over their own lives or, put another way, a laissez-faire attitude that life is hard and must be accepted as such.

• Glorifying the struggle, or acknowledgment that there were hard times in the marriage but pride at having gotten through them.

• Marital disappointment and disillusionment.

Husbands' Reactions Important

Among the couples who divorced, the husbands were likely to be "low in fondness, low in we-ness, low in expansiveness, while also being high in negativity and marital disappointment," the researchers said. For the wife, important predictors of divorce included being low in togetherness and high in marital disappointment.

In examining the couples' approach to problem-solving, the researchers found the husband's actions—specifically a tendency to withdraw from the argument—were most predictive of divorce. The tendency of husbands to stonewall also was related to the development of health problems in their wives, Gottman said.

The Seattle psychologist is also studying 140 newlywed couples to assess their marriages before and after they have children and to develop a way to predict early which marriages are likely to fall apart soon.

"I've been amazed that even in newlyweds there is an enormous range in the quality of the relationship—the degree of caring, anger, bitterness, even hostility that couples express," he said.

Reprinted from the *New York Times.*

10/28/92

Dear Jack,

By the time you get this letter there will be just three weeks until your Thanksgiving holiday, then just three more weeks until your Christmas break . . . and that, my son, will conclude the first half of your second year at Cate . . . ⅜ down, ⅝ to go. God, how time flies!!!

So, just *six short weeks to go*. Learn all you can, study hard, make the most of every minute you have in that *six short weeks*. You will only go this way but once, make the most of it!!

And now to the nits and nats:

1. Thanksgiving. . . . I'll pick you up at Cate Tuesday the 24th at 2:30. We'll drive home and then your mother will pick you up at 5:00 Wednesday. You'll spend four days with her and I'll pick you up at 6:00 Sunday evening. I'll drive you to Cate Monday afternoon, the 30th.

2. Christmas. . . . You are to spend December 19th to Christmas Eve at 6:00 with your mother. Therefore, I suggest that *she pick you up at Cate on the 19th*. I'll pick you and the kids up Xmas Eve and you'll be with me for ten days (Christmas and New Year's) and I'll drive you to Cate Monday the 4th.

Then, old boy, you have 9½ weeks until your spring break (March 10th–28th).

So, as I said, put your heart and soul into *learning,*

learning, learning, for the next three weeks. . . . Then take a week off and do it again for another three weeks!! If you do, Jack, you will prosper. Concentrate on learning and the grades will come. Count on it!!

I am so heartened by the fact that I know that *you are trying your best.* At last, you are doing all you can, and you have shoved your whole stack in! And I am so proud of you!! Know that!!

And Jack, *I am looking forward to Christmas!!* We will be in our new condo and may spend some time in Ventura. The little guys will be with us. You will have your driver's license so you will be free to come and go as you please. It should be wonderful!! Let's make it so . . . for everyone!!

     Love

        Dad

10/29/92

Dear Jack,

I must tell you that I was very pleased that you told me you wanted to try dope . . . *not* pleased that you wanted to try, but pleased that when you did, you would tell me. Note I said "when" you tried it, not "if" you tried it.

Several people think I'm nuts!! Phil, for example, asked me if I thought it was OK for you to try heroin, or coke, or suicide, or bank robbing. Obviously, that answer is "NO."

Let me set forth several things that I believe:

1. Pot is *very* dangerous *when used frequently.* It causes personality change, loss of memory, damages your chromosomes (thus your children), and it causes lethargy. . . . All that is proven!! But I don't think one-time use, "trying it," is the end of the world. *If* it is *one time* and *one time only*!

2. I think that a parent that is *unrealistic* is *stupid*!! Kids *will* experiment with booze and *will* experiment with pot. It's the nature of a teenager to want to experience things for himself/herself and make his/her own decision. Parents better accept that. They did it, their kids will do it. That *does not mean* that experimenting with "heavy" drugs is OK.

3. I think that a parent, sooner or later, has to decide whether he/she trusts their child's word, and *more importantly, I trust your word* and *I trust your*

judgment. At some point a parent has taught the right values or they haven't. . . . *I hope I have.*

4. To *use* any substance . . . booze, nicotine, drugs or whatever, is sickness if it is done to alter mood or mind. By that I mean that to drink coffee to "get started in the morning," or to drink to "relax at the end of the day," or to do dope to "be social and party" or take sleeping pills to "help me get some rest," *is sick. How much determines how sick!!*

So that kind of says the main things I believe. Now then, as regards to my son, whom I love more than life itself, let me say this:

A. You will never be able to say, "I have never smoked dope." If you are truthful you will say, "I tried it once when I was a sophomore in high school because I wanted to learn firsthand what it was about. I never tried it again." You know what Bill Clinton's experiment with pot did to him.

B. You will break the law. I'm glad you will not be in a public place where you could be arrested.

C. Using pot is not "cool," "mature," or "in." . . . It is *dangerous*, *stupid*, and usually indicative of weakness and/or a social and/or personality problem: *I don't want you to ever use pot twice* and I hope you won't stay around when *other people* are using it.

D. I see no major problem with a beer or two on a social occasion *provided that*: (1) you are not in a public place where you can be arrested for breaking the law and (2) you are not planning to drive a car or be with a driver who has been drinking. I see a *major problem* with drinking to "get high" or to "get drunk." Anybody that *purposely "gets drunk" is sick.*

E. *One single use*, "trying," "experimenting," or otherwise, *of coke, heroin,* or *LSD is like playing Russian Roulette*!! There is no such thing as "casual use" of hard drugs. . . . If anyone even pulls out some coke in your presence, *you leave. Period!!*

F. Actually, I am glad you want to have the *one-time* experience of smoking pot. Now it won't be the "forbidden fruit" with all the attractiveness thereof. Now you *personally* will know what it is. Now you can say, "I've tried it and I don't choose to use it again" . . . and Jack, *I truly hope that is the case.*

    I love you
                    Dad

11/8/92

Dear Jack,

It's Sunday, Jan is reading, the kids are out playing, and I'm at my desk catching up on "stuff."

I've enclosed yet another article from the paper about a couple of kids killed in a car during "the deadly time" (that's 10:00 P.M. to 2:00 A.M.) . . . and like I said, it *will* come out that they were drinking. I'm not saying you have to be off the road during "the deadly hours" but I am saying that police statistics show that 7 out of 10 drivers on the road during that period *have been drinking.* Further, if you've been drinking the odds go up geometrically that *you will be in an accident* and *maybe killed,* or worse, crippled for life. Look at Allan, *he has never recovered* and it was his friend who was killed, *not him.*

On a more pleasant note, I've also enclosed the floor plan of our condo. I really think you will like it. Besides, the southeast part of town is going downhill fast!! Not a week goes by, *literally,* that there isn't a murder during a robbery at one of the quick markets on Peach or Chestnut. Peterson's is going broke and most of the stores, or at least a lot of them, around Kings Canyon and Clovis Ave. are boarded up. Anyway, Outta here!! It's a whole different world on the north side of town. Most of your friends are there, all the activities are there, all the good restaurants are there, etc., etc.

Well, old boy, that's about it for now. Just *two weeks* to go until your Thanksgiving break. . . . Study hard andmake the most of the next two weeks. *And* you need to visit with your math teacher. I know you are reluctant to ask him for special help but *do it!!*

Love

Dad

11/15/92

Dear Jack,

Just one more week of school until your Thanksgiving break!! Boy does time fly!! Make the most of this last week, study hard, *participate in class*, and meet with your key teachers on anything you think you need some help with (i.e., developing your ideas in history and some of the concepts in math). I'm sure you will do well but *bear down this last week* while most of the kids are coasting up to the break.

It's Sunday morning, I've read the paper, had my coffee, and I'm about to do the day. Lots to do, but I wanted to get a note off to you first.

It looks like (about 99%) the house sale is going through and the condo purchase is also going through. The house closes the 20th and we will rent the house from the new owner for the two weeks until the condo deal closes and we can move in. We can move in at noon, December 1st.

If you could ask Cate if you could return a day late so you could help me move *that would be great*!! I've enclosed a time line for the break and you can see how critical the schedule is. If you could stay the extra day *without missing important studies* it would sure help me out.

Today I'm going to spend all day packing up the books . . . what a chore!! Can you believe that we have *over 130 feet of books* in this house?!?! God! It's amazing how much "stuff" we have acquired in the last six years here. You know, Jack, this house has been good to us. I have a million wonderful memories here as I'm sure you do, too. But it's time to move on and start a new chapter in our lives.

As I'm writing this letter there are at least fifteen kids outside standing around two cars with their hoods up. Evidently they spent the night next door and when they started to leave, their cars wouldn't start. Boy am I ready to move!!

Brian is going to announce for mayor the third of December. I think he can win!

Oh yes, one more thing . . . Derksen [the watchdog—ed.]: What the hell are we going to do with him? Do you think one of the faculty members at Cate would want him? You should ask.

Jack, you *cannot believe* how many balls I have in the air: the Education Foundation (I haven't told you about that), the Dinuba development, the Ventura franchise, the gold company (I'll tell you about that when I see you), the art store (same!), the HSA marketing of franchises, etc. The money is coming in and going out and I'm trying to make sure it equals out!! No small job. . . .

I'm going to be in Los Angeles and Ventura on Wednesday and Thursday (18th & 19th). If you have a game one of those days, I'd like to see it. And perhaps we can have dinner Wednesday evening. Call me by Tuesday evening to let me know.

Oh yes, one other thing. . . . The two academic medals that were on your Computech framed letter, I took them off and put them somewhere but I can't remember where (old age I guess). I'm sure I didn't lose them, I just can't find them. . . . Do you know where they are?

Now to Ventura. The way it looks, the franchise business will be up and running by January 1st and Jan and I are expecting to have a place in Ventura by then. That means that Jan will move out of El Segundo and up to Ventura. We'll spend our Christmas with the kids, probably in Fresno at the condo, but we may go to Los Angeles for a couple of days. You might give some thought to what you would like to do during the Christmas holidays.

Well, old boy, that's about it for now. I miss you a lot. I love you and I believe in you. I know you are doing your very best in your schoolwork and I'm proud of you.

Love

Dad

11/20/92

Dear Jack,

One of the hallmarks of being a teenager . . . and by the way, do you realize that you are *over halfway* through your teenage years? . . . is being "moody." Whether it's hormones or the stress of growing so much and learning so much in such a short period, I'm not sure, but all teenagers are "moody." Fortunately, your affliction has been milder than most. *But* you sure can get moody and when you do, you usually take it out on me. Example: Parents' Weekend when you saw your grade reports you were a total asshole for a couple of hours. Example (much less): Last Wednesday you bombed your history test and were anxious about varsity lacrosse. You were not your most pleasant self.

So what's the answer? (What's the question?) First of all, realize that your moods swing and realize how pressure affects you. You are a fairly intense, competitive kid. That's great!! It pushes you to greater performance. But the downside is that your highs are higher and your lows are lower than some kids. You have to understand yourself and understand pressure and learn to handle stress without chewing your fingers to the bone and turning into a raging asshole on occasions!!

Your father is, of course, the *perfect example* of someone who is total grace under pressure, *never* nervous, *never* high-strung, just steady all the way . . . and if you believe that . . .

Anyway, give some thought to the situation and work on the problem. It's *not* out of control, but does bear some thought . . . enough said.

Strange how things go . . . and the twists and turns of life. George is quitting art, says it is too much "hassle" and he needs $10,000 *badly*. A *big* show of his fell through due to a death in the promoter's family, etc., etc. Anyway, Arthur and I bought his *entire stock* of paintings . . . wholesale!! We'll place them, on consignment (that means we get paid when they sell), in galleries around the state and collect over the next period of time. It could take a year or so to sell them all and will take a month or so to place them. Anyway, you and I will get to pick one out and have it for our home, as will Arthur. That will leave 15 to sell and recover our $10,000 plus profit. . . . Anyway, we'll see how it goes. Crazy, huh!!

I'm looking forward to next week's drive home and the day we will have together. I'm going to get up very early Tuesday and drive to Los Angeles for a meeting. After the meeting I'll drive to Cate and be there about 2:30. We should be home about 6:30 or 7:00. Please have your friend picked up *here* about 7:00 so we don't have to make two trips across town that evening.

It might be a good idea to make your driving test appointment on Wednesday before your mother picks you up . . . OK!?

That's about it for now. It's Friday and I have a bunch of meetings before I pick the kids up at 5:00. This will go off with the mailman and you will get it Monday or Tuesday. Hope you call over the weekend so you can say hi to the kids.

Love

Dad

12/1/92

Dear Jack,

Seldom am I not proud of you. *Seldom* do you not display a good set of personal values.

Well, Jack, Sunday evening and Monday morning you accomplished a rare event: I was *very* disappointed in you. Your attitude was *selfish* and *unappreciative*.

1. Jan worked her *ass* off over the Thanksgiving holiday, packing everything up to move, including a lot of your stuff, including even your model airplanes. You uttered not one word of thanks to her. She left her work early the day of your driving test and drove all the way to Fresno so you could use her car for your test. Not a word of thanks from you. She changed her Monday plans, then went out of her way to accommodate you. Not a word of appreciation.

2. I have been busting my ass to get things together. I won't even trouble you with what *I've* been through and what *I've* accomplished but it's been a bunch, believe it!! And it included working my schedule around picking you and your friend up at Cate and making sure you had your driver test at the best time for you. Not a word of appreciation or "thanks Dad," much less any sensitivity to what I've been doing or accomplishing or what I've been through.

Now, Jack, teenagers are not necessarily noted for their unselfishness but *you overdid the privilege*! I can't believe you refused to break down your bed and told *me* to do it later!! Jack, you spent more time admiring your new ($55) shoes than talking to me. When I tried to talk to you about some of your teachers' comments . . . they were *consistent* in *all* saying you need help in study and learning habits . . . you blew me off . . . I was disgusted!!

In short, Jack, you came off as uncaring and ungrateful. I noticed it and Jan noticed it. And it hurt me deeply!!

Love

Dad

12/10/92

Dear Jack,

Let's take a moment and talk about us. Jack and his Dad, a father and a son.

We have been very close since you were a little boy. We have shared many experiences, from Alabama to the zoo to the divorce. Those experiences have helped to cement our relationship. I worked very hard as a father, a single parent, to work with you on your development and your values from the time you came to live with me to the time you left for Cate. I think I . . . *we* . . . succeeded . . . you as a son, me as a father. You were, and are, a fine young man of good character and good values.

The decision for you to go away to boarding school, and all that discussion implied, was a conscious one on my part. Obviously, I was concerned with your getting the best education possible. And that certainly was not available in Fresno. But even more than that, I felt that I had given you all of the basics that I could and it was time for you to have exposure to other influences and role models . . . and there was (is) the rub.

Selfishly, I wanted you to stay at home. I didn't want to lose the closeness we had always had, and even more so, I didn't want to lose the *daily* contact with you and the ability to counsel with you on a daily basis. I also didn't want to lose the enjoyment of daily contact with you.

But, in addition to the education and role models and contacts you would have at boarding school, I felt that for you to *really* develop yourself, you needed to be *out of the nest* and a bit away from a strong, dominant father.

Jack, I think we made a good decision. But I'm a bit bothered by how things are going right now. . . . You are sixteen, the usual time a young man turns away from his family and more toward his friends and his own activities. But your being away at school at this critical time in your life compounds the situation insofar as I'm concerned.

Jack, do you realize that you have not written me a single letter in *five* months? Do you realize that we seldom talk on the phone more than once or twice a week and that's really only for a couple of minutes and is usually *very* superficial? And you haven't shown *any desire* to come home for a weekend visit.

Jack, I don't know how you feel . . . maybe I do or you'd call more . . . but I miss you and I feel that our relationship is suffering. *I feel that both of us are losing something!!*

Jack, relationships between two people, boyfriend and girlfriend, husband and wife, or father and son, take work. You have to *communicate*, share and just plain spend time together. Otherwise the relationship withers and dies. I promise.

OK, old boy. It takes two to tango. I've said my bit, the ball is in your court.

      Love

        Dad

P.S. I had a good talk with your history teacher. He could not have been more complimentary about you and your progress as a *scholar*. Congratulations!!

I know how hard you've been working and it looks like it is really paying off!!!

THE NIGHT I ALMOST DIED
AN ENGLISH COMPOSITION ESSAY
BY JACK BROOME

It was no surprise last New Year's Eve when my dad walked into my room and said, "Jack, you're not going to go out tonight with your friends. It's New Year's Eve, and there will be nothing but drunks on the road. I want you in the house by eight, and you aren't going to leave after that. But, you may have people spend the night, as long as they arrive by 8 o'clock." This was not a new story. For years, my dad had not let me go out on New Year's Eve. The only difference last year was that I had a car. So, I gave him a nod of agreement, and went about my business.

It was about 7 o'clock when I ended up calling a girlfriend of mine and asking her if her parents would allow her to spend the night. They never had before, and we didn't expect that they would on that night. But, contrary to what we expected, her parents gave her permission to spend the night. A little stunned, I left immediately in order to pick her up and be back by eight. When we returned to the house, my brother and sister had prepared a movie, and we all sat down with some food and began to watch. When my dad came in the room an hour later, at about 9 o'clock, we were completely wrapped up in the movie. He looked down at me and casually told me that a friend of his was going to come by and take him to a party that was only a couple of blocks away. He said that he would try to return by 11 o'clock in order to celebrate the new year with us. Something inside of me wanted to tell him not to go, but he was the authority, and I figured that his judgment was better than mine. I just hoped that he knew what he was doing. When his friend arrived, I said hello, and then gave my dad a big hug before he walked out the door. Heading back in to watch T.V., I tried to push aside my unwarranted worrying. He had to know what he was doing.

When the front door didn't open at 11 o'clock, I must say that it did worry me a little. When my dad says that he will be somewhere at a certain time, he is never late. But, being that he had not said that he would definitely be home, I tried to convince myself that he was having a great time, and would get home as soon as possible. At about a quarter 'til twelve, my brother, sister, and my friend, MaryAnne, began pulling out the party hats and whistles. We had finished the movie by that time, and MaryAnne had turned on M.T.V. They kept pulling me off of the sofa, and putting stupid hats on my head. They kept asking, "What's wrong, Jack? Why don't you try to have some fun?" I realized that I was being a bit of a party pooper, but something inside of me just wouldn't let me relax. Something just didn't feel right.

I was glad that MaryAnne was there, because without her, I don't think that my brother and sister would have had much fun. She kept them screaming and dancing for hours. When the countdown was finally over, I finally had my way, and everybody calmed down. I got my brother and sister to go to bed, and MaryAnne and I headed to my room. MaryAnne told me not to worry about my dad, and that he would surely make it home alright. I finally said that she was probably right, and that we should just go to bed. On that note, we got on our "bed clothes," and got in my bed. (Don't get me wrong. We were just friends!) We had only been talking for about ten minutes when the phone rang. I was praying that it was my father. Instead, I picked up the receiver and heard a man say, "Is this John Broome's home?" "Excuse me," I said, "but who is this?" "This is the Fresno County Police Department," the voice said. During the couple of seconds that my heart stopped, a thousand things must have gone through my head. Why the police? Did my dad do something wrong? Did somebody do something to him? What the hell is going on? I was completely shocked! After a couple of seconds, the man resumed, "Your father has been in a little accident. He is at the hospital getting checked out, but he should be home within a couple of hours. Just go to sleep, and he will be there in the morning." I then made a mistake that I have had trouble living with ever since. I trusted what the man was saying, and I hung up the phone. A little dazed, I returned to the bedroom and told MaryAnne what had happened. A few hours earlier I had been told not to go out because it was dangerous, and now the person who told me this had gone out himself and gotten in an accident. Anyway, because it sounded like a little fender-bender, MaryAnne and I pushed it aside, and began talking again. We must have been up for hours that night just relaxing and sharing thoughts and experiences with each other. I don't know at what time, but we finally fell asleep very late that night.

I was awakened by the telephone ringing by my bedside. Half asleep, I picked it up and mumbled something into the phone. When the lady said that she was with the police department, I was too asleep to be surprised. It was not until about five minutes after the conversation that her words sank in. She said that the accident was a little more serious than I had been told, and that my dad would remain in the hospital until later that day. She told me that he would give me a call later. Just before hanging up, I got the name of the hospital where he was. When the conversation was over, I headed straight for the shower. It was like the warm water of the shower suddenly cleared the confusion out of my head. My mind began to function again. I knew that I could not sit by and wait for a phone call that may or may not come. I had to do something. Jumping out of the shower, I threw some clothes on, and set to work. Everyone else in the house was asleep.

I called the hospital and asked for a man named John Broome. The phone rang, but it was picked up by a woman instead of my father. I asked her what the hell was going on. She said that she was a nurse, and that she could not tell me anything about the patients. After much arguing, the woman would still tell me nothing. With a few words of frustration, I slammed down the phone. Having an idea, I ran around the house and woke everybody up. I piled everybody in my car, and sped out of the driveway. On the way down the road, I told everybody the basics of what was going on. I told MaryAnne that I was going to drop her off at her house, and would call her later. From her house, I headed straight for the hospital with my brother and sister. Upon arriving, I told them to wait in the lobby. I found out where my dad was, and took the elevator to his floor. The nurses there told me that I was too young to go in and see him. I told them that I was the only one home at the time, and that I'd be damned if they weren't going to let me in his room. I was half-way down the hall when I finally finished my sentence. I now wish that I had walked into his room a little more prepared.

Rounding the corner, I could not believe what I saw. My father was strapped down to some bed that kept tilting back and forth, and he looked almost dead. His body was covered with blood and gashed up. It was the first time that I can remember in which I could not hold back my tears. All of a sudden, his eyes opened a little, and he reached for me. I took his hand, and as I looked down upon him, I realized that without him, there could be no me. I finally got my mouth to ask him what had happened. Although he was completely drugged up on morphine, he somehow managed to talk. He told me that somebody had hit him, and that a girl in his car had died. The word death hit me like a brick. The next thing that I remember is being pulled off of the floor by about five nurses, and being placed in a chair. Later I was told that I had fainted, and had hit my head on the sink on the way down. After sitting there for a few more minutes, I told my dad that I loved him, and that even though I had to leave, I would return very shortly. After being told that he would almost surely live, I headed for home. On my way, I dropped my brother and sister off at my mom's house.

Once home, I called my dad's fiancée in L.A. She flew into Fresno about three hours later. It felt great knowing that with her there, I was not the only one to make decisions. After visiting my dad again, we both set about calling doctors and friends, and trying to make sense of the whole mess. We learned that he had broken his 2nd and 3rd vertebrae in his neck, and that he was extremely lucky to be alive. Three days later, my dad refused to stay in the hospital any longer. He had a Halo put on, and was allowed to return home. I stayed home for a few extra days of vacation in order to help take care of my father. I ended up doing all of the things for him which he had once done for me. I cleaned, fed, and shaved him for many days. Because of his broken ribs, he could not even cough without my help.

It turned out that on the night of the accident, my dad had been driving his friend's car home. It was a small Mercedes coupe, and his friend was in the passenger seat with a girl on his lap. My dad was driving because he was the only one who had not had anything to drink. They were hit from the side in an intersection by a car going about 55 m.p.h. The driver was drunk, and he ended up dying in the accident also. The only thing that saved my father was his seatbelt. It is thought that the girl in the car is what saved my dad's friend.

To this day, I cannot fathom the whole incident.

There is a feeling of guilt deep down within me that keeps telling me that I could have prevented the whole thing. Why the hell did I not keep my dad from going out, just like he had done for me? I cannot believe that while my dad was in a hospital bed, almost dead, I was lying in bed with a girl completely enjoying myself. I keep feeling that I should have acted when I received the first phone call from the police. I'm quite sure that if it had been me in my father's shoes, he would have done something immediately. If my father had died that night, I cannot even think about what I would have done. If he had died, a huge part of me would have died also. The whole incident made me realize exactly how close I am to my father. Although there were many things that I did wrong that fateful night, the incident did show me how mortal we all are, and how much life really means.

1/19/93

Dear Jack,

Just a quick note.

I'm on the mend. I have good days and not so good days, but overall, I'm improving greatly. The biggest problem is trying to sleep with this contraption on my head . . . that and getting tired *really quickly*. I really shouldn't complain, though. It looks like there is no permanent damage and I survived a *double* fatal accident. The forced inactivity is driving me nuts but that too may be a blessing, I've had some time to really think about a lot of things.

Jan has been an absolute saint. She has bathed me, wiped my butt, cooked meals, cleaned house, and has done it all with love and not a single complaint. And it hasn't been any fun for her, believe me.

Love

Dad

1/22/93

Dear Jack,

Jack, I'm very concerned about your test scores on verbal ability. That is the *main* entrance requirement for Cal, Stanford, and USC. You should be testing *much better*. There is some problem and/or reason why you aren't. We *have to* find the reason and correct it. That means talking with the learning specialist at Cate, *in depth*. You have to cooperate with this, old boy, it's your future. . . . OK? . . . OK!!!!

Vince got the bookshelves up in my study and this last weekend Derek and Steph put the books in.

Jack, I hope you wrote Phil a thank-you note for taking you back to Cate. That was *very* thoughtful of him and cost him a day off work. As I said, I hope you showed the class to write him a thank-you.

This is all for right now. Believe it or not, a two-page note pooped me out.

Love you, son

Dad

2/4/93

Dear Jack,

I went to see Dr. Slater today and the prognosis isn't as good as I had hoped or as bad as I had feared: My neck is healing, but not really quickly. It's a bit out of line, but not so bad as to require surgery or to create really major problems later. Slater said he would have me out of the "Halo" next week (thank God!!!) and put me in another type of brace that holds my head rigid with a chin rest and a back-of-the-head rest, but will allow me to wear clothes, sleep semi-normally, shower, drive, and otherwise get around normally. God, I can hardly wait!!!

The bad news is that it looks like the other driver didn't have enough insurance coverage so *there will be no quick, adequate cash settlement.* And in all likelihood there will be no advance on settlement. My lawyer will have to locate assets and sue for them. That's a long process, even if we succeed. So I have to get back to work and *crank on like a bear.* I'll be in OK shape but things will be close. I guess the lesson *again* is that there is no free lunch, no pennies from Heaven, no Lotto jackpot. And maybe that's for the best. Anyway, on we go.

Jack, I need to know the date of the RLS game. If there is any way in hell to be there, *I'm going to be there.*

Well, there are just *five weeks from today* until your spring break! Hard to believe that your sophomore year is going by so quickly, but it's already *half over*!!! Work hard these next five weeks, it won't be long. And let me know what you would like to do on your break. With the snow what it is, you will probably want to go skiing. Let me know what else. (Well in two weeks, it will be spring in Fresno and *it's up to you.*)

I hope you thanked the Farbers for picking you up and I hope you do something special for them. They are really great people and they care for you.

That's about all for now. Remember that Derek's birthday is the 13th and Valentine's Day is the 14th. Don't let Derek's birthday pass without his brother re-membering him. And Beth deserves a Valentine's Day card as does any other special girl/woman in your life.

     Love

        Dad

2/8/93

Dear Jack,

Haven't heard from you in several days so I thought I'd drop you a note.

I just got a call from Dr. Slater. He is going to take the "Halo" off tomorrow morning at 8:30!!! I had hoped it would come off today but no such luck. I'll have to wear another type of brace for another month, but at least the head bolts will be gone. I'll be able to shave, shower, and get a haircut. . . . Ah, life's little pleasures!! Believe it or not, I've been in this thing for 40 days (that's 5½ weeks!). Boy, will I appreciate my health and vitality in the future. I guess you never appreciate things until you lose them.

I just read a couple of *absolutely startling* statistics. Jack, believe it or not, only *3–6% of all high school graduates* in the United States graduate with the ability to write a letter, read an article in a newspaper, and do even simple math. Another 45% can barely write, even a note, maybe read a menu and do simple addition!!! That means that 50% cannot even do that!!! I just couldn't believe it . . . but the source is good. Without dwelling on the tragedy of American education (which the article says is the worst performing in the Western world), think a moment about Jack Broome: seven years of a top-flight grammar school (after three years of a *great* preschool), then two years of the *very best* that the public system can provide, *then* four years at one of the top secondary schools in the country. Jack, do you ever think how fortunate you are? You should thank God every day for your blessings.

Jack, let's talk about "kissing up." I guess there is no worse thing one kid can accuse another of than "kissing up," and it was when I was your age and I'm sure it was when *my* father was your age. The implication is that by affecting a (false) fawning attitude toward someone in authority and being especially courteous or obsequious, some special favors, *not earned,* will be granted. When I thanked the counter girl at the x-ray lab, you accused me of "kissing up." That was an overboard use of the term because I was, obviously, not trying to gain advantage, we were *leaving.* Jack, I was being *sincerely* thankful and expressing it! A lot of people are thankful for good service or kindness and they never express it . . . so what good does their appreciation do? You know, you might make someone's whole day with a little special "thank you."

Jack, you have never raised the topic with me so we've never talked about it, but I'm sure there is a lot of peer pressure at Cate *not* to "kiss up." I'm sure that includes spending special tutoring time with teachers, eating with teachers (or upperclassmen), or being especially communicative with teachers or administrative people. Jack, if that's the case, it's bullshit!! My experience is that the marginal kids are the ones that put the greatest pressure on the top kids not to "kiss up." And that's based on pure jealousy!! And envy!! Jack, be courteous, be gracious, be thankful *and express it*!! If you are criticized for it, fuck 'em!! Spend as much time as you can with your teachers, that's what they are there for.

Jack, do what is right!! *That rule will never fail you,* I promise. And don't bow to peer pressure on unimportant stuff. Your friends will still be your friends and anyone who isn't, wasn't worth it in the first place. Believe me, you're better off. And if a teacher gives you the benefit of a doubt or an extra quarter grade because you are a *nice, appreciative, communicative, enthusiastic* kid, well, so be it!! Besides, being nice is good for the soul.

Jack, I love you and I miss you a lot. Call me when you have some time and drop me a note when you can take some time for your old dad.

      Love

          Dad

2/19/93

Dear Jack,

I was pleased to get your call this morning, I hadn't heard from you in a week. You seemed relaxed and happy and we had the best chat we've had on the telephone in quite a while. . . . Great!!

I can always tell when it's spring. The *Fresno Bee* starts printing Blossom Trail maps, and Jack starts talking about tennis and mountain bikes.

I was quite disappointed to hear that Beth had taken up with another guy so quickly. . . . Tacky!! I really had expected more from her. I'm glad you seemed to be taking the whole situation so well. *Remember*, Jack, *never* a bad word about her *to anyone*. Be friendly toward her and speak well of her. Be a class act! I know you will be.

Remember to write Steph a note. She is your only sister, and the quality of the relationship she has with you is, to a great degree, *up to you.*

—Well, I just received *two*, count 'em, two letters from you. The first dated 2/2, though *postmarked 2/15*. . . . The second letter was the *nicest, longest* letter I have ever received from you. . . . You can't know how good those two letters made me feel. . . . Jack, you're great!!!

Some quick responses:

- Yeah, you have your dad back . . . a bit more thoughtful and careful and appreciative than before, but back nonetheless.

- I'm glad you appreciated Jan and my coming over to RLS [School—ed.]. . . . It was worth it.
- You haven't mentioned what public service Cauz's group is doing.
- Great minds think alike; I started talking about summer in my last letter. You mentioned it in yours. Yes, let's have a great ⅔ of a summer (⅓ you will be in Spain).
- Yes, Jack, sometimes you do come off as an unappreciative little (not so little anymore) shit. I cannot tell you how much your expression of thanks meant. Not so much for me but more for you!!
- You might want to send Jan a note. Yes, I'll tell her you appreciate her, but she would like to hear it from *you*.

I don't know if you have been following this last week of Clinton and his "plan." Jack, this man is the *slickest politician* I have seen in my lifetime, really. I have never seen a politician break promises, pervert facts *knowingly*, and otherwise con the public with such dexterity. Example: In his speech he made a big deal about "cutting costs to reduce the budget" and the public cheered!! The fact is: year 1 there are $2 billion in cost cuts and $68 billion in *new taxes*. The *new* spending is $98 billion so we go in the tank $30 billion *more*. The out years aren't a lot better. . . . I fear for our country. Be alert, Jack, and don't be conned by Clinton. He is just another tax and spend, cut personal freedoms, hurt the productive members of society, pander to each vocal special interest, Democrat, only smarter than most. *His words mean nothing.*

Speaking of politics, Brian is doing really well in his race for mayor. Patterson is backed by all the developers he has sold out to and so he is flooding the airways with commercials and has the most money. Humphrey has the minorities and the unions. Brian has a great base of middle-class taxpayers. March 2 is the primary (I don't think anyone will get 50% so there will be a runoff in April, I think). The question is, who will be the top 2?

I've enclosed a planning sheet for your spring break. I've noted some scheduled things above the line. You can fill in your desires below the line. *Problem:* I think you are supposed to be with your mother the weekend of the 13th & 14th (I guess a school activity excludes that) and the weekend of the 27th & 28th.

Anyway, you will probably want to schedule some time to go up to Sierra Summit, and if you want you might think of having a party with your old friends while you are in town. Other than that, I'd like to block out a couple of specific days to spend with you (we might drive to Yosemite and have lunch with Ed one day) and you should block out a day to finish up your room. Also, Phil would like to have lunch or dinner with us and we should spend a morning looking at Explorers. . . . *So, plan it out!*

That's about it for now, Jack. I love you and I miss you and I'm proud of my son, growing so big, so fast, and so well. Thanks for the letters.

Love

Dad

2/22/93

Dear Jack,

I just spent a great weekend with Steph. We took walks, went to Malibu Grand Prix, fed the ducks, went to Millerton Lake, and just generally laid around. I wish you had called while she was here, she wanted to talk to her big brother. Janis was in Florida at a meeting and Derek chose not to come, so it was just Steph and me. . . . She is such a joy (she reminds me of you).

Jack, you would not believe it but, *overnight*, it's spring!!! The flowers around our condo are blooming (not the roses yet) and they are just magnificent!! The blossoms in the orchards are incredible!! This is the really great season in Fresno, it is so pretty. I don't think the blossoms will last until your spring break, which is too bad.

Dick came by last night. He had worked all day Saturday and wanted a little company. He is very close-mouthed about his personal life, but I know he is having severe problems at home. He doesn't want advice or to talk about it, so all I can do is just be a friend. Maybe it is because he has no son of his own but he certainly cares a great deal for you. He thinks you are a fine young man, which you are, and he would like to be your friend. Dick is a bit different in some ways but you could do a lot worse than to listen to what he has to say.

The bookcases are now in, and the TV table has been cut down to fit the corner (you probably hardly remember the corner). Anyway, the place looks great!!

I'm a little bit confused about your history course this

semester. You took Far Eastern last semester; what is the subject for the second half of the year? Also, what are you studying in each one of your courses? Jack, take a minute and give me a detailed answer on this. I'm really interested!

Jack, I'm still concerned about pot at Cate. I know Clark is a regular user and I guess Erin is too. Is pot being used by very many kids? Is there an "in group" of pot users? How does their use affect them, personally and socially? What is the general attitude of the kids at Cate toward use of dope? I have expressed my *very strong feelings* that, now that you have experimented once with pot, "tried it," that you now refrain completely in the future, for all the reasons that we have discussed. Will the fact that you don't use affect your relationship with your friends that do? *Please* answer these questions so I can have a better understanding.

—You just called. I'm glad you had a fun weekend. I'm only sorry you could not have found a little time to call while Steph was here. I think it is important that you invest some time in your relationship with the only sister you will ever have.

You mentioned your conversation with Beth. I like Beth. I think you should do what it takes to remain friends with her. You need to *really realize*, I'm sure you do, that you and Beth have a *fundamental* difference in a *basic* set of values: Be it due to insecurity or because of her parents' divorce when she was so young, or whatever, Beth *wants a relationship*. On the other hand, for whatever reason, because you are a man, or whatever, you want her, but *you don't really want a relationship*. You want more in your life than just a girl. Beth wants a guy, and *that's enough*. I'm really not sure you *ought* to give it all up for a single relationship, but the choice is yours. In any case you need to *fully realize* the *fundamental difference* in where you and Beth are coming from.

Jack, it's all part of growing up, which you're doing, and by all signs, doing well. Take it all in your stride and it will work out fine.

I love you, son

Dad

2/23/93

Dear Jack,

It's hard to believe that just four weeks ago writing you a one-page letter tired me out so that I had to lay down and rest. I'm improving every day. Today, Dr. Slater took the back brace off my neck. He says I'll get the chin rest off in 2 or 3 weeks. He says I will be a bit sore and will lack lateral neck mobility for some time, but that I'm progressing *very* well.

I've prepared a time line of your summer vacation. As you can see, your thirteen weeks are pretty well broken up between Spain, your mother, and Steph being with us. I really think you need to spend *as much time* with *Steph* as you can. Therefore, I would suggest you do your hike with your friends right after school. If that's too soon, you could take some of our time with Steph here, or take some of your time at your mother's. I need to know soon, though, so I can make reservations with Ed. Then there is *our* hike: I've thought up a *great* one!! How about *just you and me* going out to Devil's Postpile up over Mineret Lake, down to Shadow Lake and out. That's three days, two nights. Jan and Steph (or even one of Jan's friends) could drive us to Devil's Postpile, drop us, spend a couple of days relaxing at June Lake while we hike and then pick us up at the Agnew Meadow trailhead. It's an absolutely breathtaking hike, off the main trail, on a trail that not many people use or know about, and I think *you would love it*. We'd have to carry sleeping bags, the bug tent, and our food. You'll carry more than your share!! Anyway, I'd enjoy it. It would be your first hike outside of Yosemite.

We also ought to plan something special to do while Steph is with us. She is not a really great hiker, but she does like the mountains. One thing we *will do* in the early summer is go down the Kings River in the raft. Jack, you wouldn't believe the amount of water in the dams. They will be running over the tops for the first time, *this summer*. That means a great outflow on the Kings River.

We could do several days at Jan's condo at Del Mar in August while Steph is with us . . . again, you'll have to let me know so I can make arrangements.

A couple of other thoughts: Here at the condo, you will have use of the little pool here, or the big pool at Woodward Lake, as well as the tennis courts, and use of the boats at Woodward Lake. In addition, the park is a block away.

Now then, your working this summer: I think I can get you a construction job where you can work when you are available. If so, you'll have to let me know how much you want to work.

As to your gold-plated, high tech, whiz-bang, top-of-the-line, time-of-your-life, "I'll take care of it like a baby, though I let my other mountain bike rust in the wind," "I want it so much" new $1,200 mountain bike: I would suggest that you call the bank and open a special savings account. I then suggest you go to Gram, your mother, and Dave and solicit contributions to the cause. Then I suggest you figure out what the balance is you need and how many hours of work will be required . . . then do it!!

Do you know who really misses you? . . . Frazzle!! She sleeps on your bed, sniffs your clothes, and otherwise is a mess. Damn, that little girl needs love!! But damn, she sure *gives* it!!! She is absolutely the *sweetest little person I've ever met*!! She has been such a consolation to me these past seven weeks. . . . She couldn't talk, but she always gave love and seemed to say, "I care."

For the last seven weeks I haven't been able to sleep, either in the Halo or in this new harness. *So,* I've been up until 2:00 A.M., 3:00 A.M., or even 4:00 A.M., until I finally got so damn tired I *did* sleep. Then I'd sleep for 2 or so hours, wake up, and then sleep again for 2 or so hours, until 7:00 A.M. or so. Then I'd doze off two or three times during the day. *So,* now my internal clock is totally out of whack!!! I don't get tired until 2:00 A.M. and I wake up at 8:00 A.M. . . . I'm going to have to get back to normal!! And think, this is a problem! It could be worse!!

That's it for now, Jack. Focus on your studies!! Lacrosse and mountain biking and girls are great but you're at Cate for an education!! And your grades will get you into a great college. So don't lose sight of what's important.

I love you, son

Dad

4/5/93

Dear Jack,

Are you "exceptional"? Do you consider yourself "exceptional"? Do your peers, your teachers, and others, consider you "exceptional"? . . . And is it important to be "exceptional"? And *what is* "exceptional"?

I don't mean "different." Everyone is "different" in his own way.

An "exceptional" young man *has exceptional qualities*. He will grow up to be an exceptional man. Top colleges look for the "exceptional" young person to admit to their schools. Companies look to hire "exceptional" job candidates and then they "fast track" them to top management positions. Law firms and investment banking houses look for "exceptional" people. Girls look to date and marry "exceptional" boys. So *it's important to be exceptional*!! Life is easier, you have more opportunity, and everyone wants to be with you *if you are "exceptional."*

So if an "exceptional" young man has exceptional qualities, what are they and how did he get them?

First of all, most "exceptional" men *weren't just born that way*. Yes, some rare guys have it all and were born that way. *Most* had some qualities to start with, developed others with hard work, and usually had someone who *cared about them and guided them* to be "exceptional."

So, again, what are the qualities that make an "exceptional" young man?

In *random order* some are:

1. *Looks.* . . . You don't have to be "drop dead handsome" to be "exceptional." You don't have to wear the most expensive clothes or the latest style. You hope to be born with at least moderate good looks and *that's hereditary. You* were born with *moderate good looks.* What is important is cleanliness, good grooming, and developing a *personal style* that *fits* and you are *comfortable* with.

2. *Brains.* . . . Again, you have to be born at least *able to learn.* That's hereditary. There are a lot of kinds of "brains," once you pass the basic threshold of being "able to learn": There are specific smarts (like Alie's ability with math). Some people are creative, some can retain by rote and are said to have a "photographic memory." Some people have exceptional ability to reason and are innately logical. Some people have just plain old "common sense." Some people are great with languages, they just have a natural facility. Jack, you are above average in intelligence, *not brilliant,* but plenty smart enough to learn. But you will always have to bust your ass to be "exceptional" in the "brains" department. You do have common sense and you were raised with books, reading, intellectual curiosity, and a love of learning. *That's a plus.* Also, you have been sent to the best schools, where your "brains" could be developed, and *that's a big plus.* You haven't really found your special ability, your niche. But Jack, that will come. In any case, you know you have

to *work at it* to be "exceptional" in the brains department.

3. *Personality.* . . . Are you likable? Are you a leader? Are you respected? Some guys are just plain *liked*. Some guys have the personality and the personal magnetism to be attractive and liked. You were *born with that quality*. But you will also have to cultivate the ability to call people by name, smile at people, remember to be interested in *them* and ask about *them* and *be nice* (you sometimes call that "kissing up"). . . . You will have to develop the attributes of leadership and strength (without being overbearing). And if you have values and if you are *true to your values* and if you are consistent, people will respect you.

4. *Initiative.* . . . The guy that always *puts out*, always *tries his best*, always is *ready to go, he is exceptional*.

5. *Athletics.* . . . You were born with a great physique. That was hereditary. You aren't a world-class athlete, but you certainly have natural ability and whether it's tennis or golf or lacrosse, you are pretty damn good. If you concentrate and really try, you can be better.

6. *Character.* . . . It's part of having values that make up your personality, *but more*!! You can always tell a man (or boy) with character. One is solid, the other is weak. Casey *has it*, George and Nathan *don't have it*. Character is the outer reflection of inner strength based on knowing who you are and what you believe and *living it consistently*.

7. *Sense of Humor.* . . . Maybe this is just part of personality, but I think it's *more* of a *category by itself.* Can you see the humor in any situation? ("I've got you right where I want you!!") Do you have the ability *not to take yourself too seriously?* Are you the one that breaks the tension, but *isn't the clown?* . . . *That's exceptional.*

8. Other important items to be that make a person "exceptional":
   - Giving, helpful, thoughtful
   - Generous, kind, *never mean*
   - Not wasteful of time, money, or things
   - Interesting and *interested* . . . learning all the time . . . growing all the time
   - Brave, courageous . . . *without being reckless*
   - Forgiving, not petty!!

Jack, I'm sure I've missed a lot of things, but you get the picture.

You can be "exceptional," Jack, *if you choose*!!

As I've told you, you're in the driver's seat now. I really can't *make* you do anything or *into* anything. *It's up to you!!* You can build any kind of "Jack Broome" you want. Or not! And you will be the one who lives the rest of your life with who (and what) you have built and *the consequences* of what you have built. And it happens day by day in *little* increments. Just like the man who lifted the calf over the fence every morning and after a year people wondered how he could lift that big bull over the fence. . . . It happened day by day and he didn't notice it.

Jack, I know you will choose to be "exceptional." Day by day by *doing what's right* and building the very best Jack Broome that there can be.

I'm with you, old boy, and very proud to be your dad.

Love

Dad

4/13/93

Dear Jack,

Thanks for calling Jan this morning. . . . That birthday call from you meant a great deal to her. She loves you very much and has done so much for you, that call showed that you care for her and appreciate her. . . . Great!!

But even better news from your call was your report on your grades!!!! *Four A's* and *two B's* (one of which was a B+ and the B was an honors class) *ain't shabby*!!! Not at Cate, for sure!!! I could not be more proud of you, Jack . . . it shows that *you have really focused, you have really been working,* and *now it pays off*!! The real payoff, of course, is that acceptance letter to a top college you choose!

Anyway, I'm really happy for you, you have really delivered. That makes any sacrifice to send you to an expensive boarding school *well worth it*!!

It's only a week and a half to Parents' Weekend. . . . I'm really looking forward to seeing you. You're a great kid, Jack, and a great son. I miss you so!!

      Love

          Dad

JUNIOR
YEAR

9/9/93

Dear Jack,

I want to thank you for a delightful drive to Ventura, your company was most enjoyable, and for taking the time to have lunch with me. It was very gracious of you to spend the time with your sainted father (and not rush him once!) when you had friends to catch up with and a room to put away. I appreciated it a lot!!

I sat on the beach for a while and napped and read, then drove back to Fresno. Glad to have you happy and back to school and sorry to be without your company.

You have probably settled in by now and have everything put away neatly and orderly. *I sure taught you that!!*

With things squared away, Jack, start your academic year with a bang. Each year you have started slowly and *really never caught up.* . . . Make this year different!

Jan called from "high energy" Mt. Shasta! She said it was really beautiful, she bought a bird book and a history book of Mt. Shasta, and she will be home Saturday. She wanted to know if you made it to Cate OK and wanted me to tell you she loves you.

Frazzle misses you!! She has been in your room, on your bed, crying like she was being strangled. I really wonder how much she senses about your coming and going. I suspect that all she really knows is that she misses you and *you ought to be here*!!

Jim Price called and wanted to know if you had made it back to school. He has his new office all set up and may be ready to open for business by October 1st. He wanted to be remembered to you. I told him how much you appreciated the loan of his pack and tent.

Later. . . .

I'm sitting here reading the newspaper, watching the birds eating their seed, and having my coffee. *Damn I miss my son!!* It's hard to believe that the summer is over, you're back to school, you're an upperclassman, a junior at Cate, and it's *ten weeks until your Thanksgiving vacation.*

Enjoy the most wonderful time in your life, Jack!

    Love

        Dad

9/9/93

Dear Jack,

Let's talk about decisiveness, aggressiveness, and focus:

I read the yearbook section on lacrosse. *Your name wasn't even mentioned.* I told you last year that you *didn't keep your eye on the ball,* and you *weren't focused on scoring* and *didn't dominate* or *intimidate* the opposition. You *didn't get in there and scrap. You didn't hit.* You said you were only a sophomore and you didn't want to "showboat." You said your time would come. . . . Well?

I listened to you call Appleton's office for a phone number and name. . . . *You didn't get it. I called and got it!* Why? I took charge of the conversation, knew what I wanted, and *politely insisted* on getting it. *I got it.*

You choke on tests. You are shy about moving in on girls (hell, Donna *got you, you didn't get her*).

You have the looks, you have the brains, you have the charm. But you don't have the self-confidence and I can't figure out why! I think there may be two reasons: (1) mental attitude and (2) technique. And *I think you need practice.*

1. Mental attitude *is a lot.* Oriental martial arts are to a great deal *visualizing success,* whether it's breaking boards or taking down an opponent. The guy that anticipates failure, *fails!!* I'm not talking about unrealistic optimism, I'm talking about *realistic acceptance* of *success, in advance,* then making it happen. You remember how

"psyching up" prior to a tennis match helped you win. When you thought you would *lose, you did.* When you thought you would *win, you did.*

2. Technique is a lot.

A. In lacrosse you have to look at your opponents and *realize, really realize,* that you are faster, just as big, and have better skills than they do. Further, you have to really realize that they are probably looking at you and are *scared* of you.

B. At your first meeting, you have to *intimidate* your opponent. Look him in the face with a cold stare. The first time you have contact, hit hard, even harder than you have to, *knock him on his ass*!! After that, he will respect you and fear you. And *then* you have him by the balls.

C. Preparation . . . preparation . . . preparation . . . and *more* preparation!! The guy who is prepared will be confident and he will have the right attitude to succeed. *In sports or academics!*

D. The guy who *"acts"* decisive will be *treated like he has already won,* so he will win. When you have a telephone conversation, you identify yourself *proudly,* you ask the other person to identify themselves, you *state your purpose,* you assume it will be met, you *proceed to satisfy your purpose,* period!! When you are going into a room you pause at the door in silent announcement of your presence (while you scope the room and decide where you want to be), then you enter the room and *walk directly to where you want to be*. People will notice you are decisive. You don't wander into a room as if you didn't know where you were going and might not even belong there. You don't start a conversation *hemming* and *hawing* like you were *ashamed of yourself*. You respect *your* time and *theirs* and get to the point. . . . *Then they will respect you!*

NOTE. . . . I'm *not* saying to be *arrogant, self-absorbed*, or an ass. I'm *not* saying to be loud or "pushy." I'm saying that in a *dignified, quiet, forceful way* you can assert yourself!

E. In academics you need to use lists, time lines, memory tricks, etc., to be sure you *really have the picture*. . . . You really have the point.

There are a million other techniques that will establish to *yourself* and the *world* that *you are there to get it done, to be the winner you are*. Discover your own techniques. Develop your own style.

But remember to get *decisive, be aggressive*, and *focus* on your real *objective*: A goal, to get the A, to learn, etc. . . . *You will!!!*

Love

Dad

9/12/93

Dear Jack,

On your Father's Day card last June, you said something that has bothered me ever since. You said when you grew up you, "wanted to be just like your dad." . . . Wrong!!!

Jack, first of all, always be your own man. Learn from others, your father included, but *be you*.

Second, you should want to be *much better* than your dad. And you should want your son to be much better than you. That's what America is all about . . . the chance for each generation to build on the previous generation and *be better, have more,* and *contribute* more.

My job, as your father, is to pass on all that I know and the benefit of all I am to you so that you can climb on my shoulders and be much better. There are lots of stories of fathers that are jealous of their sons and try to hold them down. Pity those men and never be one of them. Cheer your son on as he, with your help, passes you by!!

Jack, I have certainly tried my best, as a man and as a father. And I appreciate it so much that you would choose to emulate me. But realize all the mistakes I've made and learn from them.

I failed at my marriage. Perhaps I picked the wrong woman, but if I hadn't, I wouldn't have you. But, even so, I'm sure I could have tried harder, given more, been more understanding, and been more patient. . . . So learn. Take your time and pick the right woman. Make sure you are ready for marriage and all that will make your marriage work. Then do what is necessary to *make* your marriage work.

I have been bullheaded all my life. I've stood for principle when it wasn't really necessary, and cut my nose off to spite my face. I've told off some people I really didn't have to, and later they got my ass. I've often thought results were what counted and diplomacy wasn't necessary. . . . Bad mistake!! I've often let my ego get in the way of what should have been my focus on getting real results. I allowed myself frequently to drift in my career, going from opportunity to opportunity rather than setting a course, establishing goals, and then making my own opportunities. Quite often in my life, I was having such a good time that I lost sight of the solid goals I should have been pursuing. I always acquired assets I wanted (i.e., books, art, etc.), rather than staying liquid enough to take advantage of investment opportunities that required ready cash.

In short, Jack, I've made a lot of mistakes. You should learn from them and not repeat them. One of the things I've tried to do has been to give you the benefit of those mistakes by advising you of a better way.

So, son, realize your dad has tried his best, has done OK, but certainly not as well as he could have, and has feet of clay. Love him if you want, but always be your own man and march to the beat of your own drummer. . . . Be better and hope your son will be, too.

Love

Dad

9/26/93

Dear Jack,

It was great to see you yesterday but *I left a bit concerned.* . . . You looked *very tired and run down.* I realize you have really been "booking it" these past couple of weeks. I also realize *your diet isn't the greatest.* But there have to be some things we can do to improve the situation:

1. I think you need to take some protein pills and you need to insure a proper intake of the food groups, even if you have to "eat around" the grease & other stuff Cate offers that really isn't good for you.

2. *Sleep is important at your age. You really can't "book it" until 4:00* A.M. *and then get up at 7:00* A.M. *for school.* That's taking it from your *needed sleep.* I think you have to find other activities to take the time from. You really have to *plan your time* and *budget your activities.* And *if you still can't make it without dangerously cutting back on your sleep, then drop a class.* Otherwise, you'll get run down and then sick and *that really is inefficient use of time.* Anyway, things ought to lighten up a lot after your outing week. We'll talk more later.

I read your composition about the accident, and Jack, *I was very touched. Very!!* You know as close as we are *there are things we don't really talk a lot about.* Time and distance intervene. (That's why I want you to write *more letters in more depth.*) One of the things we really haven't talked a lot about is your feelings about the accident. Some of the things you mentioned in your composition I really didn't realize:

First of all, *in no way were you responsible for my decision to go out that night.* I knew it was dangerous, but I thought that to go eight blocks couldn't really be that bad. . . . Boy, was I wrong!! Jack, you weigh the cost/benefit or risk/reward, or other factors, all through your life and *sometimes you win* and *sometimes you lose.* I've lost a few and won a few. *That one I lost* and it could have been the whole ball game. But that was fate and "God's plan." (More on that in another letter.) It certainly wasn't your fault and *you shouldn't assume responsibility.*

Second of all, in any activity of life, there is "20-20 hindsight." *In retrospect, there is little we couldn't do better.* Jack, that's why *experience* is so important and why you are lucky to have a father that loves you and will take the time to *guide you from his years of experience* and why you are lucky (and wise) to care enough about your dad *to listen. Not all boys have that.* I didn't, and so I had to make a lot of mistakes and learn on my own, *the hard way.* You certainly learned a lot from the whole accident experience.

The thing that really came through in your composition was your strong relationship with your dad and your love for him. *You have never expressed* those feelings so strongly *to me before.* Jack, *I really am lucky* to have a *son like you.* And *I love you in the same way.* If something ever happened to you, I'm not sure what I would do.

Oh yes, one other thing we have learned from the accident: *You violate your principles at your peril!* The principle was: *Don't go out on New Year's, it's very dangerous.* Well, I violated my own principle and I *paid the price.* Principles have good reasons behind them. . . . Obey them!!

I mailed a large envelope to you when I got home . . . the one I forgot to bring from Jan's. It will be waiting for you when you get back from your Outing Week, as will this letter.

I can understand that you want to return with your classmates. I only offered to pick you up because I thought you might want to spend an extra evening with Steph and me, and have a chance to rest & clean up.

Anyway, Steph and I will drive down to Cate *Saturday* and take you out for a birthday dinner. You can invite one or more friends to join us if you choose . . . Steph and I will drive back that evening so *we'll make it an early one.* I guess we'll leave Fresno about 7:00 and *meet you at Cate at about 10:30* A.M.

That's it for now, Jack, I love you and miss you a lot. I hope you had a fun time on your hike. (I'll be watching the weather but I really don't think you will need the "Long Johns" at all.)

Love

Dad

10/3/93

Dear Jack,

Let's talk about "Fate," "Destiny," "God's Will," "God's Plan," and a few other mysteries that have plagued philosophers since the beginning of time.

If God knows all, past and present and future, is omniscient, then the moment each man is born, God knows what his life will be. So if God knows what you will do, then aren't you *predestined to do it* from the moment of birth? If that is so, then we really don't have free will, and how can we be held accountable for our actions if they were predestined from the beginning of time?

If God is all-good then how can he create a Jeffrey Dahmer (the guy that killed and ate 27 young men) who is such total evil? How can evil be created by a good God?

And, if I were 30 feet more forward (about $\frac{1}{10}$ of a second) or 30 feet backward, then Burton would have *just missed our car* and the accident wouldn't have happened and Burton and the girl would be alive and I wouldn't have had my neck broken. If God is all powerful, was that accident, Burton and I being in *exactly the same place at exactly the same time*, to the foot and to the $\frac{1}{10}$ of a second, part of "God's Plan"? If so, then did I, or Burton for that matter, have any control over what occurred?

Philosophers have tortured these questions for centuries. You will address these questions in college classes if you haven't already. (Probably not, Cate isn't real big on "God stuff .") I'm not sure anyone has really come to grips with good answers, even Thomas Aquinas, the great theologian.

So, "What's the diff?" Well, you felt responsible for my accident because you didn't insist that I keep to my own principles and stay home New Year's Eve. I feel responsible for the same reason: I took an unacceptable risk and lost. But was it part of "God's Plan?" Was it foreordained that it would happen in the way it did?

Jack, I don't really have satisfactory answers to these dilemmas. Smarter men than your dad have thought about them long and hard and come up short. I will never understand, or accept, the suffering and death of an innocent child. Why do such things happen? How could a loving and just God permit it?

Or, for that matter, when people cheat or lie or steal, how can God let them win? A just God wouldn't. Or that's what I think anyway. Not that God cares what I think about the greater scheme of things. Or does he?

We can talk another time about whether God really exists anyway. I believe *he does* and is all-knowing and all-powerful (at least by any standard we mortal men can perceive).

So how did he let me have such an accident and suffer so? Was it part of the great plan to teach Jack some lessons of life and make him a better man? . . . His father didn't die, did he? I really don't know!

What I do know is this: I believe there is a supreme being.

The issue is: Was I a good man, a good father, and did I do what was right? Did I use the talents that I was given to their highest potential? Did I pass on to my son the benefit of my life, high ideals, and standards? Did I leave the world a little better for my having been alive? And will my son build upon *my* life to make an even greater contribution?

By that will I be judged. (And you too!)

I hope then God will let me in on what the plan really was. Why did the accident really happen? How did it fit into the greater scheme of things?

Think about it, son. I have.

>   Love

>   Dad

10/8/93

Dear Jack,

"What's the Point?!?" That's often the question. *Set your priorities!!*

Remember your dad yelling, "The ball, Jack!!" "The Ball." . . . Well, there again is the question of priorities, and *"What's the point?"* I was trying to get you to *go for the ball* and *score.* You were a little boy just having a good time running along, *aimlessly* with all the other little boys.

You're no longer a little boy, Jack. You're seventeen, and it's time that you can answer, *"What's the point?"* It's time that you understand what the priorities are. It's time for you to *go for the ball . . .* and *score!!*

Alie had his eye on the ball. He bought the bike cheap, sold it for more than he paid for it, bought a better one, cheap, and sold it for much more than he paid for it. And all the while he was riding a good bike. . . . *He knew what the hell he was doing.* He had his eye on the ball. He scored!! And it was all instinct.

The Tathams always had their eye on the ball. No matter what, *they've scored.* That was the point of the book I asked you to read. *That's why I asked you to read it.* And they weren't particularly polished folks either.

Now then, *what's the point* in school? . . . Learn, get the grades, prepare yourself for the next step. It ain't girls or bikes or bullshit! It's *the learning* and *the grades* and *the preparation!!*

What's the point in soccer? It's not positioning yourself, or looking good, or bouncing around. . . . It's *the ball* and *the score*!!

Sometimes, Jack, the biggest problem is *deciding what the point really is!*

You're seventeen and now *the ball is in your court.* You're not a little boy anymore *running aimlessly around the field, having a great time, without a clue as to what the point is.* Remember that little Mexican boy on your team? He always *went after the ball, got the ball,* and *scored*!! I guarantee you he hasn't had the chance to be at a Cate or even close. But I also guarantee you he still *gets the point.* And I'm not worried about him, *not him!*

So, *"What's the Point?"*

Jack, every man has to weigh the cost/benefit, risk/reward, and his own values. Sometimes it's *easy* to decide, like on the soccer field. And it's easy to evaluate your performance, like *did you score?* . . . Alie did!! Butterworth did!! Fidella Snyder's daughter did!!

Sometimes it's not so easy to decide. And I could give you a hundred examples of instances where it's hard to decide what the point is. . . . With Brian . . . "Should I stand for *what's right* or should I *win him the mayor's office no matter what?*" "What's the point?" Some calls *ain't easy.*

Since you were a little boy, I've been yelling at you. . . . *The ball, Jack, the ball!!! Go for the ball!!! Get the ball. Score!!*

> I love you, son
>
> Dad

The Point . . . continued from last letter.

Dear Jack,

Sometimes it's important to ask, "What's *his* (or *her*) point?" It's not only important to know where the hell *you* are going and what your objective is. It's also important to realize what the agenda is for the people around you. On the soccer field it's easy. They want to score . . . they want to win . . . they want to beat you . . . they want *you to lose*.

But what about the rest of life? . . . Your teachers. Do they want you to just regurgitate the facts or do they want you to *think*? Do they have an answer they expect or do they want you to reason to your own answer? What about girls? Do they want to make *you* happy, do they want to make themselves happy, or do they just want *you*? What about friends or business associates? What is *their* point? And is *their* point *mutually exclusive with a position that is acceptable to you*? On the soccer field it's a win/lose game. In life you want to avoid situations where someone has to lose in order for someone else to win. And avoid people that have to make others lose in order for them to make *their point*. In life you want to try to get into situations where you can win by *making sure everyone wins*. . . . Those are the truly *constructive* situations of life.

OK, and what if there are *two or three* points (or more) like in soccer? It's *have fun, maintain your principles*, and *win*! You have to set priorities. . . . Are you willing to cheat (give up a principle) in order to win? Is the other team? If so, will you cheat to stay even? Will you give up the fun, get grim, push the hell out of yourself and your teammates to win? What are the priorities? Again, "WHAT'S THE POINT??"

Jack, some people aimlessly go through life, reacting to situations that come along, never with a real goal or any unifying principles to guide them. *They just don't have a clue.* They never ask, *"What's the point?"* . . . They are called *losers.*

Other people *set their goals, know their values, establish their priorities,* look at the agenda of the people they are dealing with, and then evaluate their performance each step of the way. Those are the *winners.* They put themselves in situations where they will have opportunity. They *create* opportunity. They know where the hell they are headed. And they get there!!

—You just called to tell me about the death of your classmate. How tragic!! (You might go back and read my letter to you about fate and "God's plan.") I really do think you ought to drop a short sympathy note to her parents. . . . I *assure* you it might make them feel better. . . . It's the *right thing* to do. . . .

Your call underlines the point I've been making. Think how horrible it would be, in the seconds before death, to realize you had lived without doing your best, not getting the point. *What a waste.* But if the fates or "God's plan" deals you a bad hand, no matter what it is (obviously death is the worst, and three months in a Halo and another six recuperating *ain't real* good *either!*) you can be sure that you have gotten the most out of life if you have *really tried, done your best, gotten the point,* and *lived life to the fullest.* Then, no matter what, it's not so bad.

So Jack, *"What's the point?"*

Love

Dad

10/13/93

Dear Jack,

I was obviously very sorry to hear of the death of your classmate. Particularly after you had told me about her just last week. And I respect your feelings about wanting to show proper regard for her. I really think the school should have declared a day of mourning and not held classes, as you said.

I'm sorry that you did not take my advice and went up to view the open casket anyway. I really think that was a trauma you didn't have to put yourself through.

You know, Jack, each of us handles sorrow and despair in a different way. I *certainly would not* compose a song to sing to memorialize the death of a child of mine!! But maybe that made her father feel better. People really do strange things under that kind of pressure. I really think they can be a bit nuts at times like that.

You really had a *double whammie!* I *almost* died 10 months ago, and you had to rush back to school without getting the chance to release all your emotions. Now a friend *has* died. I really think some of your emotions doubled up.

Some time ago I wrote you a letter about "death." Recently I wrote you about "fate" and "God's plan." You might reread those letters.

Anyway, Jack, I realize her death was a profound shock to you and a deep experience. There are many lessons to learn from such experiences. And that's part of growing up and having experience, *you learn* and are never quite the same afterward.

One definition of learning is "the destruction of innocence." Well, old boy, a bit of your innocence has been destroyed by the first death of a friend . . . and that's learning.

I am very sorry for the pain you have experienced. It's tough as hell to go through the death of a friend. Particularly at a young age.

Anyway, buck up and get yourself back together. Remember the old Irish saying, "We honor the dead by living as they would want."

      Love

        Dad

10/14/93

Dear Jack,

I thought I'd take a couple of minutes and bring you up to speed on what's going on at Champlain Dr.

I still have some fatigue and some memory loss from the accident, but in the last two months I've improved *greatly* and I'm now capable of getting back to work with some confidence that I can perform pretty much up to my old standards.

Two months ago Home Service Alliance, Inc., asked me to resume my position as area vice president and I agreed to it. That is kind of a slow drill but it's worth the time. It's a great company.

Ed asked me to take over the financial operations of a fishing company based in the Marshall Islands (2,000 miles southwest of Hawaii). I agreed to and I met with the stockholders in Newport last Friday. Obviously, it's a turnaround situation so until I get the company straightened out, it's no secure deal. It's *Highly Speculative!*

So, I'm getting back in the traffic and more deals will come. Right now I have enough to get going.

My scholarly book on the ranchos is in final draft. It will go to the Historical Society by the end of the year. Hopefully it will open a lot of doors in the history field . . . some satisfaction, a credential, and maybe even some lecture fees. . . .

I still own the HSA Santa Barbara franchise. What I'm thinking now is to sell half of it to a working partner and help him run it. If it goes well, and I'm sure it will, my share ought to pay a good income each year. The key is finding the right working partner!!

So, Jack, your dad is back to work. I'm fairly busy, but not nearly pushed. I'm operating with *some* efficiency, maybe in some ways even more than before the accident. *Certainly I'm wiser.*

So I'm looking for good deals and budgeting my time and commitments.

I haven't redone our financial statement in *ten* months, so it's going to be interesting to see what the *real* net effect of the accident on our balance sheet will be.

Anyway, Jack, that's the picture. I thought you might be interested in seeing it all in one shot. Of course, I would be interested in your comments.

      Much Love

          Dad

10/16/93

Dear Jack,

When you come home for Thanksgiving vacation, you are in for a *real treat* . . . some of your dad's "real food." Last weekend I discovered *the very best pasta dish I have ever tasted . . . ever, anywhere!*

First, you slow-cook sausages (Italian) in garlic and some Cajun seasoning to give them a little *zing*. Then you squeeze all the remaining grease out of them between two newspapers. Then you dice them fairly small. Then you sauté in a little olive oil: mushrooms, some fine-cut red onion, 5 or 8 leaves of fresh sweet basil, a little rosemary and a little thyme and 5 or 7 cloves of fresh garlic. You then add the sausage pieces, some Trader Joe's spaghetti sauce base (it's very bland, almost like tomato paste), and some red wine. *You can't believe how good it is!!!* You'll see! You put the meat sauce over spaghetti and have it with red wine. It's about 10x as good as the best ravioli you have *ever* had!

For Thanksgiving we are going to have slow-smoked turkey breasts (big ones!) done in butter, lemon juice, and sage. And you will not believe how good it will be!! (Served with dressing, lima beans, cranberry sauce, yams, etc.) And pumpkin pie for dessert! We really ought to invite someone who would otherwise be alone, to join us and share the dinner. *We have so much to be thankful for, Jack!!* Any ideas on who to invite?

Love

Dad

10/18/93

Dear Jack,

I've enclosed a couple of things that you will find of interest. The "Please, God, I'm Only 17" is such a sad piece. But it's timely, due to Jennifer. The "Footprints" piece is more uplifting.

Not much news you haven't heard. I still haven't gotten the settlement check, but *hopefully* it will be any moment now.

I'm looking forward very much to seeing you Thursday. It ought to be a fun weekend.

Love

Dad

"PLEASE, GOD, I'M ONLY 17"
STILL TRUE

DEAR ABBY: Prom night will soon be here, and then, summer vacation begins.

Will you please rerun "Please, God, I'm Only 17"? I lost two of my best friends in a senseless car accident last May.

Maybe running that piece again will make teen-agers drive a little more carefully.—STILL MISSING CINDY AND BUD

DEAR STILL MISSING: I have printed that piece annually for the last 15 years, and each time the requests for a rerun have outdrawn all others.

Editors of high school and college newspapers have asked for permission to reprint it. And permission is always granted.

A class of teen-agers in Seoul, South Korea, recently sent for my booklet "What Every Teen-Ager Ought to Know," and wrote that they agreed that "Please, God, I'm Only 17" was the most helpful, memorable part of that booklet.

It's a powerful piece, whose author is unknown, and here it is:

"Please, God, I'm Only 17."

The day I died was an ordinary school day. How I wish I had taken the bus! But I was too cool for the bus. I remember how I wheedled the car out of Mom.

"Special favor," I pleaded. "All the kids drive." When the 2:50 bell rang, I threw all my books in the locker. I was free until 8:40 tomorrow morning!

I ran to the parking lot, excited at the thought of driving a car and being my own boss. Free!

It doesn't matter how the accident happened. I was goofing off—going too fast. Taking crazy chances. But I was enjoying my freedom and having fun.

The last thing I remembered was passing an old lady who seemed to be going awfully slow. I heard a deafening crash and felt a terrible jolt. Glass and steel flew everywhere. My whole body seemed to be turning inside out. I heard myself scream.

Suddenly I awakened; it was very quiet. A police officer was standing over me. Then I saw a doctor. My body was mangled. I was saturated with blood. Pieces of jagged glass were sticking out all over. Strange that I couldn't feel anything.

Hey, don't pull that sheet over my head! I can't be dead. I'm only 17. I've got a date tonight.

I'm supposed to grow up and have a wonderful life. I haven't lived yet. I can't be dead.

Later I was placed in a drawer. My folks had to identify me. Why did they have to see me like this?

Why did I have to look at Mom's eyes when she faced the most terrible ordeal of her life? Dad suddenly looked like an old man. He told the man in charge, "Yes, he is my son."

The funeral was a weird experience. I saw all my relatives and friends walk toward the casket.

They passed by, one by one, and looked at me with the saddest eyes I've ever seen. Some of my buddies were crying. A few of the girls touched my hand and sobbed as they walked away.

Please—somebody—wake me up! Get me out of here! I can't bear to see my mom and dad so broken up. My grand-parents are so racked with grief they can hardly walk. My brother and sisters are like zombies. They move like robots. In a daze, everybody! No one can believe this. And I can't believe it, either.

Please don't bury me! I'm not dead! I have a lot of living to do! I want to laugh and run again. I want to sing and dance. Please don't put me in the ground.

I promise if you give me just one more chance, God, I'll be the most careful driver in the whole world. All I want is one more chance.

Please, God, I'm only 17!

Reprinted from the *Fresno Bee*.

11/5/93

Dear Jack,

Well, this is a *red-letter* day! *I received your first letter* in two months! It was certainly *welcome*.

What do you mean no "big theme"? The big theme of your letter was that you cared enough about your dad to take a half an hour and write him a letter.

You mentioned your appreciation for Jan and all she does for you. . . . It might be nice to write her a letter (perish the thought) and tell her yourself. She would really value that.

As to the choice of Amy or Linda, here's the drill: Get a large piece of paper, draw a line vertically down the middle of the page, then list all their good qualities, then turn the page over and do the same thing with their bad qualities, then weigh each quality +1 to +5 and -1 to -5 based upon importance, then add the pluses and minuses, and tally the score, *then* go with how you feel. . . . *Trust your guts!!* I'm serious, you can torture the situation all to hell and back and what really counts is what you really feel inside. As far as I'm concerned, both gals sound great and I just want you to be happy with a lady you can be proud of. So go for it!!

Steph was *very* happy with the letter you wrote to her, *but most of all* she was *so happy that you wrote* her at all. Do it again!

Congratulations on your chemistry test score. It appears that all of your hard work is really paying off.

You know, Jack, I've been an "entrepreneur," a "venture capitalist," a "turnaround man" for twenty years. It's been a very satisfying career. There is some new challenge in every assignment, a new discipline to learn, a new group of people to evaluate. Certainly there has not been the security of a set career path with a single industry. But the challenge and personal satisfaction has more than made up for it. And though the odds are always against you, when you pull off a successful recovery and save a company, it's more than worth it.

Love

Dad

11/15/93

Dear Jack,

Who the hell is "*Jack Broome*"? As you are being educated and mature, you (and others) are "building" the reality of *Jack Broome*. But what are the building blocks? Well, the important ones are your heredity and your environment. Your environment is your country and its culture and your personal experiences. I'm going to deal with your country and its culture at some length in a later letter. Today let's talk about your heredity:

One of the oldest arguments around is, which is most important, heredity or environment? Scientific studies of twins, separated at birth and put in totally different life situations, but having exactly the same genes, show conclusively that the heredity dictates abilities, intelligence, and even character. Granted that there are often great differences between brothers and sisters of the same family, but that really proves the rule rather than disproves it. It is almost funny to watch hereditary traits carry through to individuals.

The same liberals that know Irish setters come to a point on a bird, *instinctively*, and Doberman pinschers attack burglars *instinctively*, and the reverse *isn't* true (a Doberman *won't point* at a bird and a setter will *lick* a burglar) will tell you heredity means nothing in humans. *Bull Shit!*

So, what is Jack Broome's heredity? Your mother's father was English, back numerous generations. Her mother was German (Ziegler). I suppose back numerous generations. Both were immigrants, or the offspring of immigrants to America.

Your father's father was English on both sides of his family back at least ten generations that I have traced. Your father's mother is English on both sides of her family back five or ten generations that I have traced. On your father's side, there were merchants, professionals, and farmers, and no criminals or spectacular successes or famous people. (Even though my mother claimed there were.) Your grandmother's family goes back to the immigration to Virginia in the 1650s and your grandfather's family goes back to immigration to Philadelphia in the late 1700s.

So, by heredity, who is Jack Broome?

He is ¼ German (Gram's side) and ¾ English (Ompa's side *plus* your father's both sides). There is no family wealth on either side (though my grandmother was fairly rich before the Depression broke her), no major scandals (though my grandmother was divorced *twice* when it wasn't fashionable), and no politicians, or none that I've ever found.

Just a line of bright, solid, fairly ambitious, hardworking people. Your maternal grandfather went to Stanford, your paternal grandfather went to West Point. Your paternal great-grandfather went to the University of Cincinnati Medical School. Your other paternal great-grandfather went to the University of Texas Law School.

Longevity is a trait on my side of your family and to some degree on your mother's. There are no genetically carried diseases (asthma, high blood pressure, diabetes, etc.) though there has been an incidence of cancer or two (not statistically significant, though; modern research indicates that there may be genetic "triggers" that cause heart disease, stroke, and cancer at predictable ages).

A love of books and learning goes back several generations on my side of your family. A love of athletics is present on your mother's side and to a much lesser degree on mine.

I'll pass on hair, height, body type, and skin, since you already know about those items.

So, who is Jack Broome before anything is written on the blank slate? What is his hereditary, if that is the predictor we think it is?

Jack Broome is a medium-boned, medium-featured man who should be 6 feet plus and have a full head of hair but not be hairy. He should have an IQ of 135 (his mother's) to 145 (his father's), which is bright, but *not a genius*. He should be fairly athletic, and like athletics, but not be a superstar. He shouldn't have any major health problems and should live a fairly long life. He should have a love of books and learning and a sense of order and tradition and a sense of "fairness." He won't have any great musical or artistic abilities. He won't have an innate sense for trading, though he could do well in business or a profession. He will be fairly even tempered. . . . All in all, Jack, that's a pretty fair start.

What you do with those building blocks is really up to you, though. . . . What you learn, and how you use your learning, really counts. . . . What kind of character you have really counts. But you have a pretty good start on life with the genes you were born with.

     Love

       Dad

11/16/93

Dear Jack,

Again the question, "Who is Jack Broome?" Among other things, he is a citizen of the United States, an American, a product of the American culture and environment in the late 20th century. So, what is "America" and what is its culture and environment?

Jack, you were born in the year of the 200th anniversary of our country's founding. I think that's important. You are an *American*, and more particularly, a *Californian*. That subspecies of American is almost a *pluperfect* American.

America is a "*place*" first of all, a place of great natural and human resources. Virtually everyone in our country came from, or is the descendant of someone who came from, somewhere else. We didn't get the rich and prosperous from everywhere, because the rich and prosperous had no reason to leave where they were. So we got the ambitious folks who wanted *more*, in a land that promised opportunity to *get more*. And we got the oppressed, people who were getting beat up where they were: racial, religious, and political minorities that wouldn't or couldn't knuckle under, and so they fled to America to seek its tolerance for diverse beliefs and backgrounds. The stupid ones and the compliant ones stayed where they were. The smart, ballsy ones came here. The great exception to that rule is the blacks in America that came from Africa. Slavery dislocated their family and tribal ties, ties that almost all other Americans have.

So, two hundred years before your birth, this nation was founded in revolution from England and based upon the experience and philosophies of the revolutionaries. Not that all of their beliefs were universally held: Jefferson was more the egalitarian, Hamilton more the elitist. Some even wanted a Royal system, but Washington would not hear of it, though *he* was to be the King!

The principles upon which our country was formed are found in the Federalist Papers, the Constitution, the Bill of Rights, and the works of such men as Locke, Holmes, and Monroe. Rights to "Life, Liberty and the Pursuit of Happiness," think of it, "*Liberty*," not so common then or even in our world today. The right to be secure in our home, the right to be armed and protect ourself, the right to our person (habeas corpus) and property, those were rights not held by many then or even in our world today. These were what men died for to found our country, and have died for over the last two hundred years to preserve it. . . . and dammit, *that means a lot*! And they died for our right to free expression. You can say anything you damn well want in America ("Short of yelling 'FIRE' in a crowded theater," as Oliver Wendell Holmes said). You can call Clinton (whatever the hell you want to) without the fear of a knock at the door in the middle of the night . . . try that in Cuba or China or sixty or seventy other countries today.

And traditions were built over the years in America. "Go west, young man" meant, "Go and seek your fortune if you have it in you." And west those ambitious young men went, first to the Ohio Valley and the Tennessee Valley, then to the Texas frontier and then as late as a hundred years ago to Oregon Territory and California. Always, the West was the place to go to seek opportunity and fortune. But most of all was the *right* and perhaps even the *obligation* to do so. And conversely, everyone knew if you didn't, *it was your choice*, you could have *if you had wanted to*, so if you didn't, it was *your own damned fault*. So America was built upon effort, sometimes failure, but even then, *effort again*. Lincoln lost *seventeen* elections and suffered business failure *twice* before he tried *yet again* and was elected president.

And we've seen waves of immigrants from Italy, Ireland, Greece, and every other corner of the earth, come to enjoy America's freedom and opportunity. Jews, Poles, Russians, Pakistanis, they all came. And they all enriched our country.

A hundred and fifty years ago a hippie in London read the works of Hegel and developed a philosophy of socialism, of state control rather than individual rights. His name was Karl Marx. Lenin studied his work and when some Germans financed his takeover of Russia in order to stop Russia's attack on Germany during World War I, one of the most tragic social experiments in world history occurred: *Russian Communism*; the Bolsheviks; "From all according to their ability, to each according to their needs" (who the hell determines "their needs" . . . the state of course! . . . sound a little like Clinton's medical plan? . . . hell yes!) . . . the great "dictatorship of the proletariat." The promise was that the state would control all, create a utopia, and then "wither away"! But it got stronger and stronger and took more and more control over people's lives and dictated every aspect of living: social and economic and political. There were no freedoms for individuals and all the benefits went to the elite, the members of the Communist Party.

But as "un-American" as everything Communism was, it developed followers in America. They ignored the brutality of Lenin and Stalin and thought Russia was great. There was no "Go east, young man" in Russia. Her frontier, as rich in resources as America, was *never* developed. When Stalin slaughtered *20 million* farmers who opposed his collectivization of their farms, American and European Communists denied it ever happened. In short, they liked the idea of an elite (*them* in *their* minds) having all the power in a society they didn't really like or trust anyway, because, in their hearts, *they didn't really like or trust themselves*!!

And the economic dislocation, worldwide, in the thirties, followed by a World War in the forties, gave the socialists an excuse to advance state controls in the United States.

New program after new program was proposed to "help people." The elite offered security in exchange for freedom and some people bought the idea. They offered benefits for chosen groups in exchange for taxing everyone "just a bit more."

And in the process, the political class gained more and more power for themselves and insured their continuation of control. In reality the political class had no respect for America, its people, or its culture, the culture that made it great.

It is interesting that, *by law*, members of Congress are

specifically *exempted* from the social security laws, the labor laws, etc., that *they* passed to govern the rest of *us*. Sounds like the controlling elite of Russia, doesn't it? Damn right . . . same philosophy. The political class voted themselves free mail, free medical and dental and drugs, they gave themselves larger and larger staffs, to a point where some staff members were no more than personal servants, and all sorts of other privileges.

And the political class was protected by their liberal allies in the media and supported by their allies in academia.

And there developed a group of what is called "in-and-outers." They are people who take jobs in government, then join lobbyist firms to seek favors from the same governmental department they were part of, then do a stint as a "visiting scholar" at a University (kind of vacation), then go back in government for a while. There are lots of these ilk that have never had a *real* job, (like Clinton) they have *always* been in or around government.

And during this period, government's cost of the total economy grew and grew to 35% or so. Again, the social programs to "cure" the Depression and wartime costs was the excuse. Then came Lyndon Johnson's "War on Poverty" ("War," again the excuse) in the early 1960s and the vast expansion of all the welfare programs. Johnson rode the post-Kennedy assassination wave to pass more and more programs.

But in the mid-1960s, a conservative revolution against the political class, and its higher and higher taxes and more and more control over the lives of the

American people (all in the name of "helping" us), was begun by Barry Goldwater, Ronald Reagan, and the *conservative* Republicans. Goldwater was ridiculed by the media and thoroughly trounced in the 1964 election. It wasn't until 1980, sixteen years later, that Reagan was elected president and a roll-back of government and its tax rates began.

I came of age, politically, under the influence of Goldwater and Reagan. I saw the dehumanizing influence of government control, how the lifeblood of commerce and individual incentive was sapped by high tax rates, and how womb-to-tomb government care took the stick (as in "carrot and stick") out of the needed human equation that builds greatness. I was considered a rebel then. When I did my radio show and preached individual rights and *responsibilities*, I was called a "neanderthal."

Things were moving in our direction until the last year of the Bush administration. Then Bush lost his courage (nobody quite knows why) and the liberal media tore him to shreds. He went from 90% approval after the Gulf War to 35% approval . . . and Clinton won. But it was really Ross Perot that did in Bush. Clinton only got 43% (his heralded "mandate for change"). Perot siphoned off the populist vote that could have gone to Bush. And Bush's lackluster effort clinched it.

So here we are in 1993. Jack Broome is deciding who he is and what he stands for. You are an *American* and a *Californian!* And that *really means something.*

And you will hit maturity in one of the most challenging periods of our country's history . . . *a crossroads really*.

First of all, let's separate the reality from the bullshit. Let's strip away some of the myth and propaganda:

1. You have grown up hearing that there is a "crime crisis" . . . *true*. You have heard that it is because society is at fault for not giving enough (through government) to some classes of people . . . *false*. We have a crime problem because the liberals have given an excuse to some classes of people to commit crime. The liberals have fostered class, race envy, and hatred, for *their* political ends, and the liberals have blocked strict enforcement of laws. *The reality is* that the welfare class, created by the liberals, and who vote almost 100% Democrat, commit most of the crime . . . along with a small number of career criminals who should be put away for good (but liberals block this as "harsh") and habitual drug users who steal for their habits. The reality is that most crime is in a very restricted area and among a very restricted group. There is *virtually no crime* at Woodward Lake. The answer is a return to the traditional American value of *individual responsibility, harsh punishment for wrongdoers*, and more "right is right and wrong is wrong."

2. You and your whole generation have been raised in an age of TV and its violence and weird values. I was raised in the age of early TV when *Ozzie and Harriet, Leave It to Beaver,* and *Gun-*

smoke were the fare, when you saw all problems solved in a one-hour episode. We had no *Godfather*, *Divorce Court*, soaps, or violent cartoons. Research shows that the more TV kids watch, the more screwed up their values are (I worry a lot about Derek and Steph and how much TV they watch). The liberals who control most TV programming have presented their perverted tastes and values (i.e., there is no right or wrong, it's all grays). TV news goes for ratings by playing up the most bizarre and violent as if it was the norm. . . . It isn't!! Businessmen (and men in general) are portrayed on TV as the bad guys (i.e., *Network* and a million made-for-TV movies about rape, wife abuse, etc.). I don't know the answer here, because I don't believe in censorship, but public pressure might help clean up the programming a bit and parental control would go a long way.

3. The schools have been taken over by the government class and the teachers' unions and no longer teach the kids. Value monitoring, "don't stress the little darlings," political correctness, and propaganda have replaced teaching the basics and insisting on learning. A return to expelling the kids who don't want to learn (the teachers' union doesn't want to give up the ADA money if a kid leaves), cutting out the crap and *TEACHING* would help. The unions want to keep kids in school as long as possible even if their education is worthless, so they won't flood

the labor force and this pisses the kids off when they find that their years in "JC" get them nowhere. . . . Let's get back to the basics.

4. You are told that the illegitimacy rate is 50% and this is a "crisis." The fact is that among blacks it's now 70%, among Hispanics it's 40%, and among whites it's 22%, *much too high* but the problem was created by the liberals who have bought the vote of the underclass and destroyed their lives with a "victim" ideology and a welfare system that is now in its third or fourth generation. . . . Tragic!!! Too often, blacks who do "make it" do so in education jobs or government jobs, many by affirmative action. They should be encouraged to go into business. The liberals tell them business is racist. . . . BS. Business just wants good people and to make money. Business doesn't care what color you are if you can do the job. And the blacks that do go into business do fine thank you.

5. Clinton says there is a "health care crisis" that he wants to solve by turning the whole health care industry over to government (18% of our economy). *There is no health care crisis!* And if there was one, you wouldn't want to look for an answer from those wonderful folks that gave us the post office. . . . The fact is that shyster lawyers' lawsuits have driven the malpractice costs up. The fact is that people are living longer and thus require more care in their old age. The fact is that minorities, lacking the education to

care for their best nutrition and health needs, require more medical care. The fact is that new technologies are expensive. But, most of all, government controls over medical care has taken the "free market" component out of medicine and that more than anything has driven costs up. So, get back to the free market, limit BS lawsuits, and keep Clinton away from it.

I could go on and on, Jack, but the long and short of it is, don't believe the crap you're hearing.

The fact is that you are lucky enough to live in the greatest land in the history of mankind. Your values and culture and traditions have made it so. People from all over the world come here and marvel and send their children to our colleges to be educated in our ways. And then they return home to govern *their* lands. America invents most of the inventions, creates most of the fashion, makes most of the entertainment, comes up with most of the ideas . . . world over! Our workers are the most productive, our companies the most creative and innovative, and our society the most vibrant . . . in the world. We beat Fascism in World War II and we beat Communism. We stand alone as the world's oldest democracy and the only world superpower, because of our culture, traditions, and values. And it is because each generation has brought in fresh blood (a new group from elsewhere wanting to be free and have opportunity). And each new group added to what they found and made us more than what they found here.

But the fight for our culture . . . free enterprise, individual rights *and* responsibilities, free expression, no special privileges . . . continues. *And you, my son, will continue the fight* because you are an American who holds those beliefs.

There will always be those who would dominate and manipulate others for their own power aggrandizement. There will always be those who do not respect their fellow citizens and their freedom (because they really don't respect themselves) and will try to curtail that freedom. They are *alien* to America and all that America stands for. They would destroy it (for its own good they will tell you). There will always be those who aspire to the government class, to the class that produces nothing. They only want to make rules for others to live by and establish privileges for themselves. . . . *They* are the *enemy* of your country!!

Jack, 2,000 years ago, the proudest thing a man could say was "I am a Roman." Today it's "I am an American!!!" Believe that. And live up to the values and traditions of America. And *mistrust anything* that is alien to that culture, our values and traditions . . . no matter who says it or how logical it sounds. If someone says to give special rights or privileges to blacks or gays or women, or any group (above and beyond the ones we all enjoy), *that's wrong* and it's *un-American*. Special rights did not make America great, *equal rights did*. Smut is smut and "Piss Christ" and Robert Mapplethorpe are trash, no matter who says it's "in" or "avant garde." When a black hits a truck driver in the face with a brick, and black Congresswoman Maxine Waters says his anger was justifiable due to the Rodney King verdict, and therefore the black should go free . . . that's plain bullshit and should be branded so. It's an insult to the 99% of blacks who are not brutal and hold the same values you do.

When the Democrats tax enterprise and success and reward sloth and lack of productivity . . . oppose them. When someone says you should believe this or that to be "politically correct" . . . stand for what you know is right and tell them the founders of your country "pledged their lives, their fortune, their sacred trust" for real values, not "political correctness."

Jack, you are an American. Stand for and protect your country and its values. Be an American and be proud of it. Learn about your country and the men (and women) who made it what it is and live up to the culture and the traditions that they have passed on in your trust.

And teach *your* son what America is and make him proud to be an American.

And try your best to make *your* contribution and leave America just a little better for *your* son.

Love

Dad

11/18/93

Dear Jack,

Again the question: "Who is Jack Broome?" We have talked about your heredity and your national origin. We have talked a little bit (a few pages' worth) about part of your environment, the *public* part, your country, its culture and values, and what that means. Now, the *personal* part of your environmental development, your *personal* self, your *personal* experiences. That's the other part of "Who is Jack Broome?"

First of all, but not in order of importance necessarily, is the fact that you were raised in an *educated environment* . . . not an "academic" world, but still a world of proper English, books, intellectual pursuits, good music (or at least passably good), respect for learning, and a respect for education. Three out of four of your grandparents were college graduates and both of your parents were college graduates and did some graduate school. You were exposed to some culture from a very early age: plays, musicals, trips to museums and art exhibitions. Your mother read to you at an early age and your home has always included a voluminous library. Your father helped you to question the world around you and encouraged you to "look it up." You traveled quite a bit, even as a youngster: to your nation's capital, to the South, etc. So you were raised to not be afraid of new people and ideas. And your father insisted that you go to the best schools and he tracked closely your academic progress.

Second, you were raised with a sense of athletics, particularly by your mother. You were given riding lessons, tennis lessons, swimming lessons, etc. You were encouraged to participate in sports. And you were fed healthy food (except for your mother's candy). Your diet *wasn't* fast food, sodas, and potato chips. You did hikes in the summer and skiing in the winter.

Third, you were raised with love and affection and a lot of attention. You never lacked a hug or a kiss or a pat on the back. You were raised with a sense of *values* and *ethics*. A lie was considered worse than a bad deed. Cheating was not allowed. Shaving corners and not doing "what is right" was not condoned. Your father taught you very early to wave at the cops (they were your friend) and took you down to the courthouse to see justice in action. And you were disciplined for infractions.

Fourth, you were raised with a sense of cleanliness and order . . . a bath every night, clean clothes every day, and a clean house and room.

Fifth, you *were not* raised to be spoiled, financially. You were always secure, and never lacked a bike, or a trip, or skis, or the like, for lack of money. And you always lived in a nice house. But money always had a value, had to be worked for, and wasn't thrown around frivolously.

Sixth, you were raised with a knowledge of God. You were taken to church and attended Sunday school. Your home was not a "Bible-thumping" home, but it was certainly Christian.

Seventh, neither of your parents abused alcohol or

drugs . . . though your father smoked to excess. Prescription pills weren't abused in your home.

Eighth, your home was always a social home, with many friends and business associates in and out.

Ninth, there were always animals to love in your home . . . from horses to pigs to sheep to a cat. I guess all we missed was a bird and a fish.

Tenth, you were raised with a profound sense of current events, politics, and the news, like Ollie North. You met local officials, state senators, congressmen, and even the president. You met generals and people in the news. You walked precincts for a city council race at the age of six and worked in a political headquarters.

But, you also were forced to suffer through the divorce of your parents. And for some time before the divorce you saw unhappiness, distance, and even anger in your home. And after the divorce you had to suffer the pain of the divorce process and the "sides" that always happen after a divorce. You were dragged into the mess. You saw mistrust, anger, perhaps even hatred, but certainly bitterness. And that certainly did not establish an example for you as to how men and women *should* relate and fulfill each other. You really need to realize how that has affected you and deal with that influence in your own life.

There is a lot you were never exposed to: You were not raised in a home where your father worked on his own car, you haven't seen drunkenness or violence in your home, nor were there company picnics and office parties because your father wasn't an IBMer or a Standard Oiler.

And you *did* have an extra dimension in your life that most boys don't get. Your living alone with your dad for four years (full-time) and part-time thereafter, and the closeness and the "man's worldliness" that entailed, has made you a bit different. From age eleven, you haven't had the "momma" influence at home. And that has made a difference in what kind of man you are (both good and bad). From age eleven you lived in a man's world, had to handle your share of the chores around the house, came to do your own laundry, went out to dinner with and even traveled on business with your dad. You met his girlfriends and even became close friends with some of his business associates (i.e., Jeff Reese).

From all of this you developed an independence, a sense of honor and values, a distinct personality of your own, and a relationship with the world around you that a lot of young men *just plain don't have.*

Because your father isn't close to his family and because your mother isn't really close to her brother, you really were not raised with a sense of close family ties. You never had (or some would say "were *never* subjected to . . .") frequent *obligatory* family gatherings and functions. And you didn't have the sense of protection that a close extended family brings (à la the Tathems or the Kennedys).

I'm sure, Jack, that there is a lot more to be said about the influence upon you of your personal environment and personal experiences. And I'm sure I've forgotten some important points. But this should get you thinking.

So there it is, Jack . . . a *partial* answer to the question, "Who is Jack Broome?" At least it's a *partial* answer *at this point in time* . . . Jack Broome at *almost* eighteen, *almost* a high school graduate, *almost* a man. Jack Broome, his genes, Jack Broome, an American, and Jack Broome, an individual . . . Jack Broome the product of his heredity, *and* his environment.

Now comes the real question . . . What are you going to do with it? Keeping your eyes on the big picture, the time line, what are you going to do with it, day by day, and week by week? . . . And to what end?

And that's not a question of what you want to "be," but what you want to "*do*." How do you want to be known as a person? How do you want to see yourself?

I think I have prepared you to begin to answer that. And *I will really trust your answer.*

>   Love

>   Dad

11/19/93

Dear Jack,

What a great six days with you! I enjoyed our drive home together, Wednesday with you, the drive to Palm Springs with you and Steph, Thanksgiving in the desert, the drive home with you, and Sunday with you and Steph. What a bummer when you had to leave this afternoon! Oh well, just *eighteen days until I pick you up* for Christmas.

Jack . . . *get me the lacrosse schedule*. Send it ASAP so I can try to make as many of the games as I can. And *get the information on your junior outing* and the 44 mi. hike so you can write it up in your hike book. Try to find a picture of you on the hike so you can put that in the book too.

You know, Jack, when you start a business you develop a "Business Plan." When you go into a game you develop a "Game Plan." . . . I'm always amazed that nobody ever develops a "Life Plan," though life is the whole ball-o'-wax, the whole enchilada. It's more important than a business or a game, yet there usually is no plan.

You told me you were concerned that you didn't really know where you are going. . . . Well, I know a lot of miserable men my age that decided to be a doctor or lawyer or whatever at *your* age, got there, and *too late*, realized they had made the wrong decision (probably because they made it too early in life). . . . Don't worry about making major life decisions now. Keep your *eye* on the real objectives at *each stage in your life*. There is plenty of time for major decisions *when the right time comes*. Actually you have *already* made some decisions: You don't want to be a doctor or an entomologist. You didn't want to be an elected official. And you're not qualified to be a ballet dancer or a professional football player.

Here is a basic "life *plan*":

age 1–5:	Learn to bathe and eat and poop without messing yourself. Learn values.
age 5–18:	Get education in the basics. Learn who you are and mature.
age 18–22:	Gain your higher education—specialize in your major in the last two years.
age 22–24 (or 25):	Get a graduate degree in a specialty like law or finance.
age 25–29:	Gain some work experience. Do an "internship," if you will. Perhaps get some Washington, D.C., experience (government and how it works and who makes it work). Perhaps get some New York experience (the major cultural and financial capital of the world).

age 29–31 (or 32):	Establish yourself with a firm or in an industry or start a business . . . using your experience and education and *contacts*. Also look for a wife compatible with your tastes, education, and desires.
age 31–34:	Start your family & build your career.

So, Jack, it will all flow. The old saying is, "By the yard it's hard. By the inch it's a cinch." Keep your eyes on the big picture, but live with the current objectives. Right now get your education and prepare for the next step. You're doing fine. Don't worry.

      Love

          Dad

11/22/93

Dear Jack,

I just received your first-quarter grades. It is clear that your load is heavy and you are doing your best. I can't ask for more. It is also clear that you could use some improvement in scholarly technique. I'm sure we can get you some help in that area. It is also clear that your performance is a bit erratic, but it is improving. If you compare your first grading period freshman year and sophomore year and then this year . . . the academic improvement and improvement in maturity is noticeably dramatic! Congratulations.

Jack, you pulled two A's and three B's. Even though the A's were "–" and one of the B's was a "–" that means if you bear down and really continue to put out the effort and since your teachers say you *are improving*, you ought to end the year with four A's and a B and *that's not shabby*.

But the thing I am most proud of is Cauz's comments (enclosed in case you haven't seen them). Clearly, my son has the values I always wanted him to have . . . particularly LOYALTY!!

Listen to what Cauz says about Jack, *my son*: "No other student at Cate has more character or sense of responsibility than he does." WOW!! What more could a father ask? Cauz says, "He is simply the best." Jack, I must tell you that those words, and *I know they are true*, mean more to me than you have any idea. Those words mean that I have succeeded as a father. Those words mean that all of my efforts have been worthwhile!! And that means that you are well on your way to having a good life. *I am so proud of you, Jack.* I can't tell you how proud . . . but *I think you know.*

I love you, son

Dad

12/2/93

Dear Jack,

Well, you've got me hooked on your damn tortillas. If you want the treat of all time, just spread a little of that jalapeño mint jelly on the tortilla before you roll it up. Now that, as they say in the South, is "mighty fine." If there is any of the jelly left when you get home, you'll have to try it.

This summer you *absolutely have to* read Rush Limbaugh's new book, *See I Told You So*. I'm about halfway through it and it is really *must reading* for anyone who wants to understand politics and government in the 1990s. It's *not* easy reading, it isn't *light* reading, but it sure is good. Really . . . I'm sure it will drive the liberals *crazy* because Limbaugh really *has their number*.

Winter sure has set in here in the valley. The temperature is in the low 30s at night and the fog sets in about midnight. Damn, it's dark. Except for the joy of a fire each night, *I hate it*. Seventy more days of it, then early spring around Valentine's Day (or Derek's birthday).

Frazzle absolutely pitched a fit the afternoon and evening after you left. She was in your room squalling like I've never heard her before. Then she roamed the house squalling before going back to your room to squall some more.

Last night I was on my way to have dinner with Ethan at 7:00 P.M. I couldn't believe what I confronted at the corner of Shepherd and First . . . an accident scene that looked *exactly* like my accident last year. Car bashed in, car rolled over, ambulance etc. . . . etc. . . . Evidently a car ran the light (going north) and broadsided a car going west on the turn. Evidently it was a fatal accident. . . . I freaked! Jack, *it's a dangerous world out there.* You have to be *really really* careful!

I just received the Dec., Jan., and Feb. Cate schedule. It looks like your first "LAX" game is at home with Midland on December 11th. Unfortunately, Steph will not be with us that weekend. The next game I see scheduled is January 22nd . . . that is a weekend Steph will be here. Jay Bligh wants to come to the January 22nd game for sure and "*might*" come to the December 11th game. Anyway, I have to be in Los Angeles Sunday the 12th, so I am figuring on being at your game the 11th. Maybe we can have dinner that evening.

That's about it for now.

Love

Dad

P.S. Enclosed is a George Will article you really ought to read! Will is *great!*

12/20/93

Dear Jack,

You're at a very interesting "Catch-22" period in your life. You're busting your ass to become something you don't know what! So if you don't know what it is, how or even *why* should you bust your ass for it?

Some kids have it easy, or at least think they do. The kids that set their sights on being a doctor or a lawyer, or Lee that wants to follow his dad in the gaming business or Martin who has a business already set up for him. But many of the kids who set their sights early find out too late that they really don't want to *do* what a doctor *does* or a lawyer *does* . . . after they *are* doctors or lawyers. And the tides can turn against a Lee or a Martin.

So what about Jack? Why should *you* bust *your* ass for an unknown (at least for now) goal? And with all the gloom and doom about our society that permeates the airways, why bust your ass at all?

I'll tell you. . . . First of all, the gloom and doom is *bullshit*, put out by black souls who are only reflecting their own inner self, or ratings-hungry promoters of the sensational, or self-serving politicians. Our society has more opportunity, more justice, more freedom than *any society anywhere, at any time in history*. We have problems and our freedoms and opportunity are always threatened by the statists who would advance government at the expense of the individual, but we have it better than *any people* at *any time*.

Secondly, and *most important, your future* is bright and

the world ahead of *you* will hold joys and opportunities you and I can only dream of now.

Think of it for a moment, in your short lifetime the computer, environmental science, new medical technologies such as the M.R.I., etc. and so many more advances, have come of age. Just in the last 2 or 3 years the fax has virtually replaced mail as the means of transmitting the written word in business. Computer modems are about to take over that and other functions such as filing taxes, filing court documents, etc. Interactive TV is two or three years away with applications you and I can't even dream of. I had a phone in my car twenty years ago when few people did and it was on a party line. And it was expensive. Now everyone has a cheap, small, cellular phone. And in a couple of years they will be contained in your watch. What does all this mean? Well, it means that in *your age* information will be more comprehensive, more available, more mobile, and exchanged at a rapidity unthought of in *my age*. Hell, when I went into business, you dictated a letter, mailed it, waited for it to get there, waited for a response to be written, mailed, and received. Now, you jot it down, fax it, and the response is faxed back in hours. Think of what that turnaround means to American business efficiency!!! And that's peanuts compared to what's coming in *your age*. In my early years platoons of draftsmen took days to do blueprints. Now CAD computers whip out fully calculated blueprints, with one man, in hours. Think of what's coming in *your age*. Jack, the technology of the Adelade Mills that we owned was around since the seventeenth century. Now that's all done with computers. Think of what's coming!

Jack, I'll bet the industry and/or technology you make your biggest contribution to and make your fortune from *may not even be in existence today.*

So how could you possibly know where you're going with any certainty? All you can know is that *you better be ready.* And what does that mean? It means you better have a good grounding in education, you better have the connections, and you better have the right mental attitude. If you have all of that, as the opportunities come, you will be the man to capitalize upon them.

So be of good cheer! Look forward to your life with the absolute conviction that as the world changes and opportunity presents itself, all your hard work now will make you ready to reap the dividends then. I know you will.

Love

Dad

12/27/93

Dear Jack,

You're at your mother's for Christmas week & my thoughts are of you. I'll write this and mail it next week so you'll get it when you get back to Cate.

There are so many things a father wants to talk over with his son. Some are personal, some are philosophical, and some are just factual reminders to put his world into perspective. Your being away at school forces me to put these things on paper. Perhaps good for both of us.

Jack, your country has mobilized for war, total war, three times: the Civil War, over the unity of the nation and, secondarily, over slavery, and both world wars, which were fought to stop aggression that was encouraged by past foreign policy blunders (i.e., lack of support for Germany's democratic Weimar Republic led to Hitler, and then appeasement of Hitler's early aggression and not sending strong signals of our intentions led to Hitler's major moves, which forced us to react). The war of 1812, the Spanish American War. The Korean War and the war in Vietnam never caused *total* mobilization. Maybe some of them should have, but they didn't. And we fought to a draw in Korea and lost in Vietnam.

As you prepare to enter college and reach maturity (presumably), *your country is at war*. It hasn't been declared, most Americans don't even realize it, and as yet there has not been total mobilization. But we are now at war, and as in World War II, we fight on two fronts. And as in the Civil War, the fight is wholly within our own borders. And as was Pearl Harbor, it's been a *sneak at-*

tack! The overriding question is *when will war be declared, when will America realize it is under attack*, and will we totally mobilize to meet the threat?

The first war we are in is *the Drug War*. Think of it, Jack: Our borders are being invaded by foreign powers transporting poisons to our cities. Those poisons kill and maim our youth and the most fragile members of our society (the poor and uneducated). The foreign powers are aided by a "fifth column" (the antiquated term for *traitors*) *within* our country (the drug bankers and pushers) that profits from the drug trade.

It is estimated that 60%+ of all crime is drug-related (from burglaries to support habits to shootings that enforce drug pushers' territories). Well over half of penitentiary inmates were convicted of a drug-related crime. It is reported that 60% of black Americans between 18 and 30 are on parole, probation, or in prison!! I'm not sure of the exact number but I know it's high. Most teenage suicides and dropouts are drug-related! The impact of drugs on medical costs is staggering! *It's War!!*

The economics of the drug trade are also staggering . . . "estimates" are that *trillions* of dollars are involved. That impact, from lost consumer purchases to bribes of officials, can hardly be calculated.

So why isn't there more public outcry? Why ain't there street marches? Why aren't politicians up in arms? Any other invasion of this magnitude would bring armed citizens into the streets. Where is the media outrage? Where are the headlines in every newspaper? Mrs. Reagan, "Just Say NO" was a joke. The "Drug Czar" role is a joke. Police efforts are being totally overwhelmed. Our borders are a sieve.

Jack, *I can't explain it!* I really just don't know. Why the hell didn't President Bush call Schwarzkopf after the Desert War and just say, "General, stop the drug traffic!!" Abide by the Constitution, but "*Stop It!!*" By God, he could have!! Is it that so many members of the media and the political class use drugs or have family members that do? Is it that the drug payoffs have gone so high? I really just don't know, I really don't.

There are those who say it's a conspiracy to destroy our country. I can't believe that. There are those who say it's only the worst of our countrymen who are affected so the politicians just let it go. I can't believe that either. Some say it is just stupidity on the part of our leaders. Some say the money is so gargantuan that nobody can stop it. I hope that isn't true, the implications are frightening.

As you grow up you may be called on by your conscience to fight in this war. You may have a role in declaring it and mobilizing your country to defeat this threat.

The second war we are in is *the fight for the soul of America*. Our country was founded and flourished for two hundred years under certain principles (I've discussed them in a previous letter). For the past forty years, little by little, law by law, newscast by newscast, the liberal elite in academia, broadcasting, and government have demeaned our principles and eroded our confidence in what made our country great. The tug-of-war went back and forth with the left making its major advances after the Kennedy assassination, under John-

son, and during the Watergate-weakened Nixon administration. We had a few victories during Reagan.

The amazing thing is that the left appears to be "fact in-
sulated"!! Socialism in Russia fell of its own inadequacies,
and the left survives! All of the socialistic "Great Society"
programs of Johnson have failed, the left survives! The
welfare state in every European country has failed, the left
survives! They are absolutely "fact independent"! Some
liberals believe that Mapplethorpe's photos of fists shoved
into anuses are art. They believe drugs are OK. They protect criminals (i.e., the Reginald Denny case), saying they
are "victims of an unjust society" instead of the animals
they are. They make businessmen the villains of every
movie and call accomplishment "greed." They try to argue
that the prosperity of the Reagan years "hurt the poor."
(BS!) They ignore the realities of the world. They opposed the Gulf War and now deny they did. They call for
full legal rights (including welfare and medical benefits)
for illegal aliens (and call them "undocumented workers"). They call "taxes" "contributions," they call vagrants
"homeless people." And they do all of this with a straight
face! They believe they are right and it is their place to
control the government that controls the people.

Unfortunately, the best of their numbers run for office
where among Republicans who dislike government, the
best of our number go into business and provide jobs
and create the wealth of the country.

Now the Democrats have the White House. And
the House and Senate, too. Now they want to disarm
the law-abiding citizens. They want to socialize 17%
of the national economy by giving the entire hospital,

medical, pharmaceutical industry and surgical industry to those efficient folks that run the welfare agencies and post office so well. Good God!!

Their sales pitch is, "We'll take care of you. All you have to do is give up a little more of your freedom. We'll take the money from those dirty bastards that make money and give it to you, just give us your vote."

Jack, this is the *war for the soul of America*. Will we continue to be a free country based on free enterprise and the individual? Or will we go with the liberal statists who believe government is the answer when *we know government is the problem?*

Again, Jack, your conscience will call upon you to fight in that war. From the time you were a little boy and I took you out to walk a precinct for Councilman MacMichael, and introduced you to politicians, I knew you would be faced with important issues as you grew up and became a man. I wanted you to be prepared to stand for what you believed in. Now you are close to manhood. Now the country is faced with war for its soul. The people in this country are conservative and patriotic. That explains the popularity of Limbaugh. The polls show we still believe in basic notions of our country. It's the media and liberal politicians that try to convince us to deny our instincts.

So: On to manhood and joining the two-front battle. Good luck, son. You're free because great men fought before you for *your* freedom. Can you do less?

Love

Dad

12/29/93

Dear Jack,

When you hear the term "National Treasures," you usually think of great works of art or certain national parks, or architecturally great buildings. What *I* think of when I hear of "National Treasures" are *people*. I think of the great leaders of our country, past and present, that have helped to make our country what it is. These are the people of arts, letters, and public affairs, that *really contribute*.

A young man (you!!) could do worse than look for the "National Treasures," see what makes these men great, and learn from them. Certainly the standards they set can provide a measure for *your* accomplishment.

Some examples:

George Will. There is perhaps no better contemporary example of precision of thought, clarity of exposition, and prodigious intellect than George Will. He cuts right through pretensions and rhetoric and bullshit. He has historical and literary perspective and cites obscure passages that underscore his points. Will's columns ought to be *required reading.*

President Harry Truman. His style was all his own: plain, homespun, and earthy. His background was not really exemplary. But, God, he had *character!* Whether you agreed or disagreed with all of his policies, *you always knew where he stood.* He didn't take a poll, test the waters, and then decide. He decided, based on basic American values, and then he took his stand, and didn't waver.

Former Defense Secretary Dick Cheney. He has spent his life in public service. He is a "no frills" guy. In a world of "workhorses and show horses" he is a *workhorse*. He is a man of totally concentrated effort. He is a man of total economy of language. Ask him a question, he thinks, he answers succinctly. The answer is *right*. He has never had a taint of scandal in his personal or public life.

Bob Hope. Here is a man who has entertained the public for seventy years and has given of his time and energy to more causes than can be counted. Every Christmas for fifty-five years he has gone unselfishly to foreign lands to bring joy to our troops who could not have Christmas at home.

Billy Graham. Through the age of shyster pastors, always out for personal gain, Billy Graham has stood for Christianity, morals, and values and never made much for himself. His crusades have brought millions the word of God.

John Kennedy. Whether you agreed with his politics, or his morals and personal lifestyle, you have to say, "*He had style.*" He had a wry sense of humor, a cheerful, self-deprecating wit, and a warmth that was absolutely contagious. He was a *leader*. And that's why he is remembered. Conservatives can't stand it, and liberals blow it totally out of proportion, but his "persona" was very special.

Richard Nixon. No matter how much the liberals vilify him (they have since he started his political career), no matter his mistakes in the Watergate affair (and they *were* serious). Richard Nixon represents *strength of con-*

viction and *personal courage* the likes of which are seldom seen. He has been *counted out* and *politically destroyed* and yet by *courage* and *force of will* and *intellect* has come back, more times than I can count. He has been a congressman, a senator, a vice president, and a president. He has written 10 or 15 books and is still (at 88) consulted by world leaders who seek his advice.

Alistair Cooke. There is perhaps no better example than Cooke of culture and breeding and intellectual curiosity.

Jacqueline Kennedy. She is a national treasure because she has class with a capital "C." She is a great mother and would have been excused if she hadn't been. Since 1963, she *never* has had an interview or a press conference. She has strength with a capital "S." She is a great example of courage, intellectual honesty, and style.

Michael Jordan. A superb athlete, a wonderful person. Jordan makes more money than Perot, is more famous than Clinton, yet he is a regular guy, a loyal friend, and a great family man. He never gripes, shows off, or plays to his celebrity. He is the pluperfect role model for black kids and white kids alike. Who has ever said a bad word about him (and been taken seriously)?

These are just a few of the national-level, world-class players. History includes Lincoln, Washington, Hamilton, Jefferson, and on and on. These were men who had the qualities and then the opportunity presented itself.

Depending upon how long he lasts and the results of his efforts, Rush Limbaugh could become a "National Treasure."

A couple of foreigners I wish were American National Treasures:

Abba Eban. The picture of civility and intellect. A totally decent man.

Margaret Thatcher. Indomitable will, a leader of high principle, totally loyal to her friends and beliefs. A great human being. The ultimate devastating argument against whining women's liberalization.

There are lesser lights who never made it to the national level or whose activities were too narrowly focused to make it to the "gold circle": i.e., Scott McLeod on purely the local level.

Anyway, son, you could do worse than to look for the "National Treasures" and see if you can emulate their qualities. . . . If you have the will and the character you can!!!

Love

Dad

1/3/94

Dear Jack,

Again comes the question . . . "Who is Jack Broome?"

I've discussed your *personal* and *cultural environment* and your *heredity*. People say they are *the* determinants of what you will become. Perhaps. . . .

Personally, I believe much more in *the indomitable spirit* of *each individual*. I've seen people with all the advantages of birth blow it. And I've seen men born with few advantages accomplish much in their personal and professional lives. In short, Jack, what you do is really at the bottom line, *up to you*!!

The deciding issues are a man's *character* and his *values*. If a man is honorable, hardworking, not frivolous, responsible, compassionate, and God-fearing, then *he will succeed* (by *any* definition). If his values are lacking, he will *fail*. . . . It may take a while, but *he will fail*.

For Christmas I gave you Bill Bennett's *Book of Virtues*. It is a book of stories of *character* and *values*. It is stories of men who matter!! (Because of their character and values.)

So, son, the ball is in *your court*. *You* will determine the course of *your* life. And the rewards of a good life and all of its accomplishments will be *yours*.

Love

Dad

1/6/94

Dear Jack,

You told me you were wondering where all this academic work was going to get you, what you would finally do, what you would finally be. . . . So what's new? That's the age-old question, "What are you going to be when you grow up?" That question is asked of middle-aged men, too!!

We've talked about the many industries where there are opportunities and the criteria to evaluate those industries. We've talked about having a "game plan" for your life. . . . OK, let's really get specific:

Your objective for the next five and a half years has to be becoming an "*educated*" man. You need to learn the fundamentals of communication, the basics of science, the essential facts about the history and sociology of the world around you, and the building blocks of society (i.e., contracts, values, arts & letters, the humanities, etc.). You will find that each academic course of studies builds on the last one and gets more specific while it takes in more complex theories and concepts.

And you have five summers to acquire some practical experience and test your abilities as well as your social skills and character. This and have some fun and see some new places and meet some new people.

During this five-and-a-half-year process, you will find yourself drawn more and more to a few areas of learning. You will also find that you will defiantly eliminate certain areas (like you already have with medicine) based on your abilities (or lack of abilities) and your likes and dislikes. You will seek summer jobs in the areas you are drawn to and thus reinforce that interest by developing personal contacts.

By the time you enter graduate school, your professional training, you will have a very good idea of where you're going, not each specific, but *generally* a very good idea.

And graduate school is the *great incubator of careers*. Successful people from business and industry come to lecture (and recruit students!!). There are seminars on different topics. There are requirements for outside research that will showcase your talents. And the constant discussions at graduate school will hone your thought process.

By the time you get your graduate degree, you will have the contacts and the knowledge to pretty much go where you want and do what you want . . . and by then you'll know what it is and what is "right" for you.

So, Jack, bottom line is: Stay focused on your *near-term* objectives, stay on course for your *intermediate-term* objectives, and you will *for sure* meet your *long-term* objectives.

I realize you have to take a bit of that on *faith*. It's hard to describe a bubble to a blind man or an orgasm to a virgin. *If you ain't been there it's hard to really visualize it!!* But Jack, *I have been there*. Believe me, you'll do fine!!

We'll talk more about the specifics of your choices and options as the years go on. And that will be fun for both of us. You have a wonderful, challenging, and rewarding world in front of you. You've always been in the *top 1 or 2 percent* and you always will be!! And that ain't chopped liver!!

Have confidence, old boy. Take life on day by day . . . *enjoy every day* and use that day to *build for the next one. And that's life!!*

    Love

         Dad

1/8/94

Dear Jack,

Well, after three weeks of absolutely dismal fog, it finally lifted and today is *sunny*. Boy, does that elevate my spirits. The damn Valley fog is just plain *depressing*. Fortunately we only have to endure it for another month, then the days will go over 65 degrees, there will be no fog, and spring will be just around the corner. Great!

I remain successful in my effort to cut my nicotine intake and detox before a final effort to quit. I'm *down* 60% and holding. An interesting result is a bit of depression and a *major* change in urine color. I've taken 2,000 mg of vitamin C for years. My body has absorbed it and my urine didn't go yellow. Obviously, the nicotine level affected it, because now *it's yellow*. (Your body expels *excess* vitamin C through your urine.)

Saturday, January 22nd, is your RLS game at Cate. Jay Bligh is planning to come to Cate for it and so is Jeff Reese. I'm going to drive down and bring Steph. Her birthday is Sunday the 23rd, so I thought we might celebrate her birthday at dinner Saturday evening after the game. You ought to decide on a present to buy for her. Anyway, you and I can formalize our plans over the next week or so.

I called Steph last night and Derek answered. He was so detached, not angry, just distant. I feel so sorry for him, and I really hope the situation doesn't degenerate into a crisis, which it very well could. I hope not. Again, if you have anything to contribute, please do so.

I'm not sure I have ever told you about the old law

school story. You and I have been concentrating so hard on grades because they are so important to where you will go on to college. You should take some satisfaction in what they say about law school grades: "The A students go on to be law school professors, the B students go on to be judges, and the C students go on to make big money in private practice." The same story is told in medical school and business school. The point is, of course, that getting grades takes a certain facility which *is not necessarily* the same facility that makes for professional success. And conversely, what makes for professional success isn't necessarily what gets the top grades. So, *there is hope!*

So, what are grades worth, other than to get you into the best schools at the next level of your education? Well, first of all it's the *habit* of succeeding. And it's the *discipline* of taking an assignment, following instructions, and fulfilling tasks. People who succeed at that in school are prepared to succeed in their life's work. Also it's the training to know how to find facts, look things up, access references, organize your thoughts, and communicate conclusions.

So keep plugging, old boy!

    Love

        Dad

1/15/94

Dear Jack,

One of the big words in our contemporary vocabulary is "STRESS." People are always "all stressed out." They are under "stress." You have said that your schoolwork has you "stressed" and from time to time you need to "kick back and relax." Your biting your fingernails is probably a sign of "stress."

OK, what is "stress"? What causes it? Is it a bad thing? What to do about it? Some observations:

1. Most stress is self-induced! We set impossible goals and then get "all stressed out" trying to meet them. We set artificial deadlines and then get "all stressed out" trying to meet them. We habitually put ourselves in the same situation (or with the same person) that causes stress. We frequently find ourselves in situations that involve great stress and we seem not to be able to extricate ourselves. (Like the people who buy a house in Orange County, work in LA, and have to endure a 1- or 2-hour commute each way, frequently tied up by freeway accidents that further delay them and add to an already stressful situation. Then property values fall, they can't sell their house and move closer to work, their wives don't want to move, and they are just plain *stressed! . . . Very* stressed!!)

2. Most people don't really understand what causes them stress. Or they *deny those causes*. Art's wife

drives him nuts, but they have kids and he can't afford a divorce and I think *he thinks* he loves her . . . so, stress. Arlene's boss was a *real bitch!!* She couldn't make decisions, changed her mind when she *did* decide something, had great mood swings, and could be really nasty, undercut Arlene with her employees, etc. . . . etc. . . . Arlene loves her job and needs her job, so she took it for two years. . . . *STRESS.* You wouldn't believe the difference now that her boss is gone.

3. Most people don't know how to treat themselves for stress. First of all, *realize* you're under stress. Take some time out to exercise or read an article or take a walk, but *break the cycle.* Then develop a game plan to attack the root causes of the stress.

4. Accept that *not all stress is bad.* Most of us accomplish the most when we are under *reasonable* stress, trying to meet *attainable* goals that are *right on the edge* of our ability.

5. Perhaps the biggest cause of stress is *the unknown:* when men are with a losing company or a declining industry and, day-to-day, don't know if they will lose their job; me, wondering when our settlement check will come; you, wondering what your grades or test scores will be and what colleges will accept you. . . . All of that causes stress.

6. Sometimes people try to affect situations they *really can't affect.* Going through a nasty divorce takes *at least 2 years.* You *can't speed it up!* When you try, you are just adding stress. Accident settlements take 18 months to 2 years. You really

can't speed it up, so *accept it*!! If you accept what you can't change, it is usually less stressful.

7. Diet and sleep affect stress, just as stress affects diet and sleep.

8. Stress reduces your immune system, and thus *stress causes sickness*. There is substantial medical evidence that stress is associated with cancer, back problems, and even AIDS and the common cold. So people ought to understand and control their stress.

9. Stress *is cumulative*. If a person is going through a divorce, he is really stressed. Then if he loses his job the stress *doubles*. Enough stress will make you sick. Perhaps that's the body's safety valve. (I'm not sure if that's the body's safety valve or if that just *adds* more stress.)

So, how to *use* stress and not let stress get the best of us:

A. Set a *reasonable diet, sleep schedule*, and *exercise schedule*. If you are fit, you are less likely to have stress take you down.

B. Set *high goals* and *reasonable deadlines*, but not so high or tight as to be impossible!!

C. *Anticipate situations* so they don't come as a big surprise and cause impossible deadlines. Make time lines so you know coming events and have enough time to properly prepare for them.

D. Be introspective enough to realize what causes you destructive stress, and *deal with those causes constructively*. I had an 8 o'clock class in S.F. when I was in college. There weren't any parking places, and rush-hour traffic was a bitch. So, instead of studying at night, I went to bed a little early, got up at 4:30 A.M., had a *no-traffic* drive to school at 5:00 A.M. and got a parking place right outside my class at 5:30 A.M. I had my coffee and juice at a coffee shop, then studied from 6:00 A.M. to 7:45 A.M. and made it to class fresh, wide awake, and *unstressed.* I left class and walked 30 feet to my car and came home. I had factored a lot of stress out of my life.

E.   *Good planning will factor a lot of stress out of your life before it even happens.* If your car is well maintained, it won't break down and you won't have the stress of a breakdown. If you keep track of what you owe and pay your bills on time, you won't have the stress of a collection call. If you deal with straight people in business, you won't have the stress of deals gone sour or lawsuits. If you go out with good women, you don't have the stress of dealing with dingbats and their antics. If you think long and hard about who you want to marry and then know her for a good while, your chances of having the stress of a divorce are minimized. If you try to avoid *stupid* things, like going out on New Year's Eve, you can avoid the stress of a probable accident and all that that involves.

So, have a good life, with enough stress to spur you on but not so much as to make you sick or be destructive.

Love

Dad

1/16/94

Dear Jack,

Let's talk a little bit about "money." Let's talk a little bit about concepts and ideas that relate to "money."

First of all, "money" is merely a *storehouse of value*. It's a *common method of exchange*. In early days "money" had an intrinsic value (i.e., gold coins) and that's called "specie." Later, paper money, not backed by any real values, came into being. Before "money" there was "barter" ("I'll give you my horse for your cow"). Nowadays, the "rate of exchange" says a bit about how much people value the currency of a nation (the dollar is "up" in exchange with the peseta).

So most people live by exchanging their labor for money, which they then exchange for the necessities of life. They can work "hourly," like a McDonald's employee, or on a "salary" like Jan, or for a "fee" like I do (some fees are "hourly" and some are "flat fees" like a doctor that charges $4,000 for a face-lift, regardless of the actual office visits or hours in surgery). In any case, it's your labor (and skill) for money. Then you pay money for food, rent, utilities, etc. . . . . That's "*earned income*."

There are other forms of money income: If you deposit money in a bank, they pay you "*interest*." If you buy a bicycle for $200 and sell it for $400, you have "profit." If you steal a TV and sell it to a fence (someone who deals with stolen goods) for $200, you have "*illicit* income." If your father dies and wills you property, and you sell it, you have "inherited income."

Now then, you have gotten some money from some source. . . . Where does it go? First, it goes to support your necessities of life. If you have some left over, it's called "*discretionary* income" (you can spend it for what you want, over and above your "*necessities*").

OK, so the *big question*. . . . What is *a necessity?* One person's *necessity* is another person's luxury. (David Gauvin thought he *had to* drive a Rolls-Royce!) Some people think they *have to* wear designer clothes or *have to* ride an expensive cross-country bike.

So, *point one:* Set your level of spending for necessities at a realistic point, based on your earning ability.

What is then left is *discretionary* or *capital*. These are *important concepts!!* If you take an expensive vacation, or eat out at an expensive restaurant a couple of times a week, you are spending "*discretionary income.*" That money then *does not* go into your savings and become *capital*. *Capital* is defined as "*deferred consumption.*" In other words, capital is money you could spend but don't, figuring you will spend it later. Savings is a form of "capital." You then put your capital to work for you and either earn interest on it or invest it and hope for profit (sometimes called "*capital gains*").

Let's say you have graduated from college and get a job at $36,000 a year. You'll pay about $12,000 in taxes, leaving you $24,000 a year ($2,000 a month). If you get an apartment for $600 a month, figure $200 for phone and utilities, $300 a month for groceries, $50 for clothes, $200 for a car payment, $50 for insurance, and $50 for gas then your *basics* are $1,450 per month. That leaves $550 for emergencies and discretionary spending (skiing trips, dates, gifts, etc.). If you don't spend it all and you save half of it, you will have $275 a month "capital," and that will earn you about $20 in interest a month.

I realize that this is a lot of detail, but bear with me. . . . If you buy a house instead of rent an apt. and if you pay the same $600 a month mortgage instead of rent (on a $75,000 house) and if you stay two years and the value of the house goes up 5% a year, you will make $7,500 profit. If you put 10% down on the house (your *capital*), you would make 100% on your money and have $15,000 in capital for the next down payment.

(NOTE: I haven't figured commissions on the sales or fees, I'm just trying to cover concepts.)

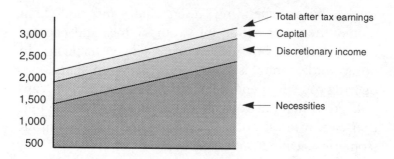

The point I'm making is that *you* set the variables: You decide what job you take, working how hard, for what total income. *You* decide what your standard of living will be, and therefore how much capital you will amass.

Now then . . . it's clear that the major variable is *not* how much you save or how low you can reduce your standard of living to. . . . The real variable is *how much money can you earn* . . . and it doesn't take a genius to figure out that salary income, less taxes, less the necessities of life during the period you earn the salary, leaving some savings to compound (deferred income/deferred consumption), isn't a sure (or quick) way to riches, and presumably, the good life.

Some random thoughts:

Alie didn't think "bicycles," he thought "money." Alie was in bicycles *to make money*, you were in bicycles *for enjoyment*. Alie will be *in everything* for money and *always looking for the angle*. And that's fine.

That desire for money *can become all-consuming*. John Garabedian went from nothing to *rich rich rich*. He cared for *nothing but money*. He was looking for deals 20 hours a day and nothing, not ethics, not friendship, not anything came in his way. When *money itself* becomes the end in itself, and *it consumes you* . . . you've lost it!

People who set out to just make money frequently don't. People who set out to do a *good job*, make a *good product*, render a *good service* . . . they make money as a natural by-product of their efforts . . . the money comes. They focus on the job itself.

Now to *debt*. Some people spend more than they make. That's the *reverse* of creating capital (i.e., deferred consumption). That's spending *before* you make it, and then you *pay interest* for the unearned money you're using.

Sometimes you borrow money to buy a property, and then when it appreciates you pay back what you owe and have a profit. But what if the property *doesn't appre-*

ciate, and you pay interest with no profit? And even worse, if the property loses value . . . that's called *reverse leverage*. And that, old boy, has broken many a real estate speculator.

What about marrying someone with a lot of family money? It seems like a hell of a lot easier than working for it. . . . Jack, *it isn't!!!* We'll talk about this another time, in depth, and if you ever fall for a rich girl, we'll *really talk about it*. But for now believe that "married money" is the hardest money a man will ever earn!!

I really ought to tell you a little about my experience and attitude toward money. . . . This is in the spirit of "don't do as I do, do as I say."

I have never been very "money motivated" per se. I've enjoyed challenges. I've worked like hell for causes (usually *for free*) that I believed in, but money *as such* really didn't move me much. I always made what I needed to make and spent what I had. I really didn't amass a great deal of "capital" though I acquired a lot of "*things*" that I wanted. Actually, your mother was a great motivator for me. She had an insatiable appetite for more and more things, and more and greater lifestyle. As a result I *had* to make more and more money to support her (and since I never got any appreciation I resented it). In the years prior to our divorce, I was making a very good living. The years of the divorce were a *financial disaster* for me (and it lasted for four years!!).

I really never operated on a financial game plan or a budget with specific goals for investment and capital return (but then I never had a father to explain all this to me). I had to learn as I went along, and that takes (wastes!!) a lot of time (life!!).

We'll talk more as the years go on about how to make money, how to use money, how to invest money, and a lot of things like that. If you're smart you'll learn from me, learn from my mistakes, and do much better in life than your dad ever did. . . . I hope so.

The object of the game is to provide a good life for yourself and your family, provide for their security, and yet not be so dominated by money, per se, that you lose your values. (i.e., Would you betray a friend or be un-ethical for monetary gain? Would you take a bribe or lie for money? I hope not.) Compare what you have to *your own life* and capacity. If you always compare yourself to others (and what *they* have) you will never be happy.

 More Later
  Love
    Dad

1/24/94

Dear Jack,

Stephanie really appreciated your call to her on her birthday. You are her big brother and she loves you dearly. Your small gesture of love and thoughtfulness on her birthday made her day.

But Jack, your call Friday really disturbed me. You were obviously down and you said your back was really hurting. Your statement "Life isn't worth living" *really blew me away!!*

Character, my son, CHARACTER!!! Perish the thought that your life would, at times, *not be perfect!* Perish the thought that you would have to endure some of the normal vicissitudes of life. It seems to me that your father damn near got killed, had to lay in a Halo for 2 months, was in constant pain, then took another 10 months to recover some of his memory and stamina. And *you never heard a complaint* . . . let alone a self-pitying whine like "Life isn't worth living." *Character, old boy!*

Perhaps you've had it so good that you think the good life is your due and there is no other life for you. *Wrong!!* Perhaps God tweaked your back to make you appreciate your otherwise good luck and health.

Jack, get on your knees and *thank God for what you have* and thank God for this *little* test of your character. And thank God for giving you a life that is *very much worth living*, no matter the minor setbacks (no pun intended).

Some news: Steph loved her birthday, particularly the fact that she got *three* cakes (one at her party, one here, one with her mother). I can't believe she is *ten* years old. She seems so grown up!

The earthquake in the San Fernando Valley was a real disaster . . . in the real sense of the word. There is much more earthquake damage than anyone ever imagined! And, as usual, someone always profits from a disaster. Jim Price's business is booming!! (It couldn't happen to a better guy.) . . . On my way to LA, the Benz blew a thermostat (scared the hell out of me). No big problem, but it sure seemed like one. Strange how people's problems are all relative . . . mine and the earthquake victims'.

Lawyers are taking *my* deposition Thursday (can you believe that!!). The notion of a drunk suing *me* is really atrocious!!

Our fishing company is off to a rocky restart in the Marshall Islands. The weather has been miserable and thus *no fish*. I hope things will improve. It was great that Ed brought this deal to me. It is a classic turnaround deal: mismanagement, lack of proper accounting, and totally optimistic projections. Notwithstanding all the frustrations, I really enjoy the turnaround business. When you can get an enterprise back on track, it is really fulfilling.

I spoke with Dr. Brown about your back. He says he knows what the problem is and he will write you a letter telling you what you need to do to correct the situation.

He also has a colleague in Santa Barbara who is a very good back specialist if you need him. But he thinks that if you do your exercises and don't overdo sports for a while, it will be fine.

   Love

    Dad

1/26/94

Dear Jack,

Well, it looks more and more like you are aiming toward a career in business. OK, I'll give you *two* initial rules. They are constants, so *learn them, use them, live by them*. All the rest will follow.

1. Business is a *people game*. Some of life's activities are technology-driven or driven by ideas but many businesses are driven by *people* and their interrelationships. So learn the players, their backgrounds, their strengths and weaknesses, and how they relate to one another. *Learn the politics* of an industry or a company. So much in business happens because certain people get along, trust each other, and feel comfortable with each other. Conversely, a lot of business *doesn't happen* because egos get in the way, or two men just don't like each other, or there is no comfort level of trust and confidence. Bottom line is: People skills *and contacts* are critical. It really helps if you know someone from your high school, or college, or graduate school, or club, and can call on a first-name basis and get an appointment or introduction or get some important information or propose a deal. A blind voice on the phone doesn't get through.

   Build your network of contacts, build your reputation for integrity. Don't make *unnecessary* enemies. Develop your interpersonal skills. When you go into a situation, know the players. . . . That's the game!!

2. Know the rules and know the ratios, you'll learn the specifics and the details later. Jack, there is so much I could say here, I really don't know where to begin.

i.e.: A low-tech manufacturing co. takes about $20,000 in capital per employee. A high-tech company can take $3–500,000 per employee. A plant needs 4–500 square feet per employee. A low-tech company will produce $50–75,000 in sales per employee. A high-tech company could produce $500–700,000 in revenue, or more, per employee. A company will spend 10% of sales on administration costs (management, accounting, etc.), 15% on selling costs, etc. So if you know 2 or 3 facts about a company, you can mentally create an equation and solve for most of the other variables.

i.e.: To get a loan you need a source of repayment, a good credit history (loans you've taken *and* paid off), a legitimate purpose for the loan, *and* a backup source of repayment in case the first source fails (i.e., assets you could sell to pay the debt). A lot of people go into the bank without their financial statement and tax returns, without assets (or a guarantor) to back up their expected first source of repayment, and then they get pissed off when they don't get their loan. . . .

They didn't know the rules of the game.

i.e.: A retail store will sell $100–400 per sq. ft. of floor space. It will pay about 50% of its sales for the goods it sells (that's called a "keystone margin"). It will pay about 15% of its sales on personnel, 15% on advertising, and about 14% on rent. Again, if you know one or two facts about a retailer you can figure out the rest. So, if you have 4,000 sq. ft. of retail space to rent, you know you're looking for a retailer who can do $800,000 a year (at $200 per sq. ft.) and thus pay $80,000 a year of rent (that's $1.67 per foot/per month). So you know that if you build a retail space for cash, out of your savings, and you spend $40 per foot to build it (a low average figure), you will return your capital in 2 years (an OK return) and then own the building free and clear thereafter. Another way to look at it would be: 50% on your money *before* insurance, property taxes, allowance for vacancy, etc. Again, if you know the rules, and you have a few of the facts, you can figure out the rest.

i.e.: A healthy company (or individual) should have as much short-term assets (cash, stocks, bonds, gold, etc.) as short-term debt (credit cards, current bills, etc.). That's called the "acid test" ratio: 1 to 1, or less, or the company or individual is in trouble, more and it isn't using the leverage it could to operate. There are many other ratios that help to understand: earnings to total debt, total assets to total liabilities. Ours is 3 to 1, net worth (including house) to total debt (including home mortgage).

Anyway, learn the ratios & the rules & you'll know business.

Love

Dad

2/7/94

Dear Jack,

Read the enclosed article and get on your knees and thank God for all you have . . . and promise God you will never again say, "Life just isn't worth living."

Then read the article a second time and think about *character*, adversity, and how to grow through adversity.

This poor girl who had it all . . . lost it . . . and gained it back. What she had was a gift she didn't earn. What she *has*, she has earned through *strength* and *character*. I sure do admire her!!!

Think about it . . . and thank God for what you have.

   Love

Dad

BURN SURVIVOR TALKS
TO TEENS ABOUT STAMINA
BY JOHN D. CRAMER

WONDER VALLEY—Heather Wyatt perseveres.

Out of the headlines for a while after being in the public spotlight in 1991 and 1992 concerning her burn accident and rehabilitation, Wyatt on Sunday brought her story of determination to the second annual Youth Action Forum.

Addressing 120 teen-agers at the leadership conference, Wyatt told how her life changed from high school track star to burn victim to young adult with hopes of marriage, children and a career as a physical therapist.

Through it all, her perseverance has remained.

"It's 1,000 percent attitude pushing you to do what you want to do," said Wyatt, 21.

A 1990 graduate of Hanford High School, Wyatt set track records, received college scholarship offers and hoped to compete in the Olympics.

But in a car accident in June 1991, she suffered severe burns on more than 70 percent of her body and nearly died.

After numerous surgeries, she has learned to walk, run, feed herself and "all the other things a baby has to learn."

"I went from life to death to living again. I still have a long way to go [probably until the year 2000 after additional surgeries] before I'm the way I used to be," she said.

Wyatt's talk Sunday ranged from the dangers of fire to an attitude of determination and self-respect that she said carried her through depression and the physical and emotional rehabilitation after the accident.

She explained burn injuries, skin grafts, operations and "learning to deal with other people who are cruel."

"Sometimes a 5-year-old will ask, 'Why are you so ugly?' . . . but older people can be just as mean and vindictive," she said.

"Please don't stare [at someone who has been burned]. Just ask them what happened if you have a question."

Although community support was widespread in the six months following her accident, only close relatives and friends have remained "true," she said.

"I'm still the snotty little brat I've always been, the stubborn hardhead, but that's the way I am," Wyatt said.

"Sometimes people ask if I'm scared, but why be scared? I'm not going to sit in a corner and shrivel and die. I want to live."

Although much of her strength and mobility have returned—she walks, dances, practices gymnastics, teaches track and drives—the burns left permanent disabilities that prevent her from exercising strenuously.

Today, Wyatt owns a house in Hanford and attends College of the Sequoias part time.

Her goals include marriage (she has a boyfriend), children, a college degree, a career as a physical therapist and establishing a foundation to assist burn victims.

"My life has gone for the better," she said. "Just remember no matter how bad it gets, it always gets better."

Reprinted from the *Fresno Bee*.

2/8/94

Dear Jack,

Character, my son, *character!!*

Four months ago *all I heard was sports*. You were bicycling. You were playing. You were working out (replay four or five times). I was concerned that your *priorities* were misplaced. Four months later God has curtailed your playing. . . . Your back went out. *Your grades are up.* You're more *humble.* You've learned a lot about your own *mortality*, and the *humanity* (*sensitivity*) of some of your friends and teammates. And you've had to come face-to-face with *self-pity* ("woe is me"). In short, God has given you the *opportunity* to get your priorities straight, realize what is of lasting value, assess your "friends," and become a *better man.* In the greater scheme of things, you have been confronted with a *minor* problem (to a 17-year-old boy, perhaps a bit more than minor). How you deal with it and what you learn and how you emerge from this *temporary setback* is *all that is important!!*

I realize that all of this is a bit philosophical when your back hurts, but *it's true.* And you need to realize it.

Jack, it's *not true* that adversity builds character. Adversity *breaks* some men. But it sure as hell *is true* that *how we deal with adversity builds character.* And it's also true that seldom will you find a man *with* character that hasn't faced some difficulties, met them head-on, learned from them, and became a better man as a result.

Like building muscle, building character is a matter of "No pain, no gain!!!"

There was an article in *Entertainment* magazine on Frank Sinatra, Jr., and his rather strange relationship with his father. I've enclosed a paragraph from the article that is highlighted. Can you imagine *yourself* and *your* father relating like that?

Jack, you need to go back to your friends and *sell* them on the books-for-Cate-Library idea. Sell them on the basis that: (1) the school ought to have the books, (2) no other group of seniors has made a gift like it before so they will stand out, (3) it sure will look good on their college aps., and (4) it will not really take them that much time to accomplish (i.e., five guys get 10 names from their father or come up with 10 names themselves). Call the ten, explain the drive, and get $200 from each of them. . . . The ten calls can be made over the summer . . . the job can be wrapped up next year . . . and *you* get the credit for having the idea, organizing it, and making it happen. . . . *DO IT!!*

It was sure good to see you. I was very impressed with Georgia, the sophomore from Orange County. She is cute, gracious, and bright . . . go for it, old boy! I hope I didn't embarrass you with my "talking eye" story. I'm sure I didn't do it very well, but it sure was funny on D.C.J. [a cable-TV comedy featuring stand-up comics—ed.]

You know, Jack, you could write your dad a letter. I'm sure you could find a half hour in your otherwise jam-packed schedule.

Only four weeks until spring break. . . . I'm looking forward to it!

Love

Dad

2/10/94

Dear Jack,

In his *Julius Caesar*, Shakespeare says, "There is a tide in the affairs of men, which taken at the flood, leads to fortune."

I've introduced you to the notion of using a "time line" as a planning tool. Now let's add some sophistication to that concept. Let's see if we can make Shakespeare's *Julius Caesar* work for you. Let's talk about *Cycles* (*not* mountain bikes) and *Wave Theory*:

First, *Cycles*. . . . You're in your junior year of the secondary education cycle. It runs September to June with marking periods, breaks, and vacations. Your ladies operate on 28-day cycles with certain predictable mood swings. You surf with the tide cycles (high & low tides and lunar highs & lows). Obviously, the weather occurs in seasonal cycles (you've seen my Fresno chart).

The political cycle starts with announcements of candidacy, goes to the June primary, has a summer hiatus, the fall campaign, and the November general election. There are the sports seasons ending in the NBA playoffs, World Series, and Super Bowl.

It seems that each industry has its own cycles: the book fair in February for the antique book trade; the fall fashion shows for the rag trade; the Oscars and its publicity run-up in the film world; the spring trade shows before the fall retail selling season, etc., etc.

Obviously, the farmers have their planting season and their growing season and their harvest season. Congress has its fall and spring sessions and its national budget cycles.

So if you "get" the concept you can pretty well plot out, well in advance, what is going to be happening *when*, and what is going to be talked about, *when*. You can even predict, within a percentage of accuracy, when natural disasters *may* preempt everything else (i.e., hurricane season, flood season, major storms, etc., etc.).

The point is, if you know what is coming, *you can plan for it*. These are obvious things, like not planning a morning flight out of Fresno (FOG!!) from Thanksgiving to Valentine's Day. Don't plan a major meeting World Series week because some people will miss it to watch the series. Plan to raise money from farmers right after harvest (when they have their money). Plan to ask a politician for a favor right before announcement time because he will want your support. Don't plan a fundraiser for the builders in April or May because they are breaking ground on projects after the rains. Don't plan much during December because people are preoccupied with Xmas parties, Xmas shopping, their kids are home from school, etc. The point is that if you use your head you can *swim with the current* and *not fight the tide of events*.

Now then, *Wave Theory*. This can be as simple as the old, "What goes up, must come down." It is usually much more complex.

Twice I've gotten involved in a business right at the start of a recession (because I didn't understand the economic cycles then) and had to work *twice as hard* to accomplish *half as much* (The Alpine Co., going into the

'73–'74 recession, and the Textile Co., going into the '82–'83 recession). If my timing had been better, just think!!

Men have career ups and downs. When they are up everybody wants them and they don't think they need anyone. But if you're the guy that offers support and friendship when a man has had a failure, he will remember, and *owe you*, when he gets back on top. And many men do (Nixon, Clinton, most businessmen, entertainers, etc.). I could give you hundreds of examples.

There is a whole school of investment based on Wave Theory. It's called the *contrarian school*. They say, "Always buy what's *not* in favor, surely it will go up. Always *sell* what's hot, surely it will go down." Again there are hundreds of examples. i.e.: After its crash you could buy Chrysler for 3½. It went to 25 in *thirty months* (that was 700% for the *smart* money; and more if they leveraged). When silver raced up past $52 an ounce, the smart money *sold* before it dropped to $5 an ounce. I bought gold at $42 in 1971 and watched it go to $650 before I sold most of what I had.

One of the major economic factors is interest rates. They *really drive* the economic cycles. I bought the Waldby St. house *and* Champlain Dr. at relative lows in mortgage interest rates. But understand that inflation *and* interests that are high *will come down*, and when they are low, *they will rise*.

Remember when you were in 8th grade and Japan was hot as a pistol and could do no wrong? Everybody wanted to take Japanese. I said take *Spanish*. Now, Japan is in a recession, the Japanese stock market crashed,

NAFTA is the hot issue, and *Latin America is the coming rage*. And *you speak Spanish*. You hardly hear about Japanese anymore. . . . That's *Wave Theory* in action.

Don't get me wrong, a lot of men have been busted trying to pick the *absolute highs and lows* ("bottom pickers"). The old saying is, "Bulls (looking for *up* trends) make it, bears (looking for *down* trends) make it, *pigs don't!!* Nobody has a crystal ball. But you can spot the *trends* and make them work for you.

OK, old boy, there is some wisdom for you, the fruit of your father's life-of-learning-by-making-mistakes because nobody told *me*. Use this as a tool & remember your dad as you "take [it] at the flood and lead to fortune" (as Shakespeare said).

> Love
>
> Dad

IT'S WHAT YOU DO—
NOT WHEN YOU DO IT

Ted Williams, at age 42, slammed a home run in his last official time at bat.

Mickey Mantle, age 20, hit 23 home runs his first full year in the major leagues.

Golda Meir was 71 when she became Prime Minister of Israel.

William Pitt II was 24 when he became Prime Minister of Great Britain.

George Bernard Shaw was 94 when one of his plays was first produced.

Mozart was just seven when his first composition was published.

Now, how about this?

Benjamin Franklin was a newspaper columnist at 16, and a framer of The United States Constitution when he was 81.

You're never too young or too old if you've got talent.

Let's recognize that age has little to do with ability.

2/15/94

Dear Jack,

I received your grades and comments today.

Bottom line is that you pulled two A's and three B's and if you *beat feet* and *focus*, you can get two of the B's to A's and finish the year with four A's and a B . . . and that ain't bad!!

As you mature scholastically a couple of areas need to be improved:

1. Dennison and Wies both point to some *erratic performance, carelessness,* and *casual mistakes.* . . . You need to *become more consistent.* That is a matter of *maturity* and *effort* and *focus.* Work on those *three.*

2. Robbins, Twichell, and Yager point to your weakness in test-taking. Jack, a lot of that is technique and *you have to get some help in test-taking methods.* A lot of that is learned skill. So get some help and *you'll add a grade point "just like that."*

The comment that I was most proud of was Cauz's. Clearly, he knows you best and respects you most. I told him *3 B's and two A's ain't "stellar."* It's good, but certainly *not great.* What was most pleasing was his high opinion of your *"uncompromising integrity."* Jack, *that's really more important than 5 A's!!* I'm proud of you! And you should be proud that he considers you a *friend.* That's quite a compliment. I'm very glad I pushed Scott [the headmaster—ed.] to switch advisers. That may have been one of my better decisions as a father.

Well, you're working hard and it's paying off. You are really bringing it together as a scholar. A couple of re-finements (i.e., being consistent and knowing how to take tests) and you will be at the top of your scholastic game and close to a straight A student *in a very competitive environment.* I couldn't ask for more than that!!

Congratulations on a good job.

Love

Dad

2/17/94

Dear Jack,

When Dallas Cowboys owner Jerry Jones was asked what kind of player he wanted in the NFL draft, he said he wanted "a play-maker, a guy that breaks the game open and makes things happen." That's also the way it is in business. People want the guy that is a "self-starter," a guy that knows what the priority is and moves in that direction *without prodding*. That translates into *leadership* because most people wander aimlessly until they see someone that seems to know where he is going, then *they follow that person*. That kind of person sets his own agenda, sets his own course, and *gets there*.

We're about Olympiced out!! It's amazing how you get caught up in some of the events: the new bobsled, for the first time in 30 years, an American design; Jensen, who won the 500m speed skating gold and broke his jinx; the absolute *speed* of Moe and Pikabo in the downhill and their personal stories; the daring of the ski jumping; the grace of the ice dancers. *Absolutely amazing*. It blows me away that there are people who will devote four years of their life to training and sacrifice, and then *bet it all* on a one- or two-minute event they can *win* or *lose* by *three* or *four feet*, or *three* or *four thousandths* of a second!! And it all has to come together at once. One slip and it's over. . . . Boy, I don't like the odds!! But then, for that one-in-a-thousand kid who stands on the tallest platform and hears the national anthem of the United States of America played as they hang a gold medal around his or her neck . . . I have to believe that it was worth it.

And, oh yes, the Harding/Kerrigan saga continues next week, when they finally hit the ice for real. Jack, you cannot possibly believe the media coverage that whole fiasco has received. . . . I'm about to throw up!!!!

I sent Cauz a note congratulating him on the basketball victory over Mission Prep and inviting him for a couple of days during spring break. You should invite him *yourself* and urge him to come to Fresno for two or three days. It would be fun.

I've enclosed an article on George Stephanopoulos. You *need to read the article*. It says a lot about values in personal ambition. Stephanopoulos is *very bright* and chose government as a career, but some of what he did applies as well to business. Remember that he is now one of the most powerful people in America, and he is only fourteen years older than you are!! As you read the article, focus on the qualities that have gotten him where he is. *Underline what you think is important* and let's talk about it when you're home.

Steph & Jan & I saw *Tombstone* today. You were right, that's a hell of a movie. I had no idea Wyatt Earp came to Los Angeles and died in 1929! The movie was set in the 1870s or '80s and they said he was married to that girl for 47 years so he must have been in *his 20s* when he was in Tombstone!! Damn!! I'm going to get a book on Wyatt Earp, particularly his later years, and find out about him.

That's it for now. . . .

Love

Dad

3/15/94

Dear Jack,

There are a lot of words that are in common usage that not one person in a thousand has given any thought to *in depth*. Over the next year I want to address some of those words and the real meaning behind them. I want to give you a starting place to formulate *your own opinions* about some words and concepts that we live with day to day.

With some insight, you will be better able to deal with the world around you and the people in it.

"Union" . . . "Strike" . . . "Picket line" . . . "Organized labor" . . . "AFL-CIO" . . . "Teamsters" . . . What do those words mean? What do those words evoke in different people? Why?

When I was your age I had to join the Teamsters Union to get a job loading trucks for United Parcel Service. Later, I had to join the Carpenters Union to get a summer construction job. I had to pay an initiation fee and monthly dues to keep my job. I couldn't figure why. I really didn't give a lot of thought to the principles involved. I just paid my money and did my job.

Most people do about the same.

Up to the 1880s workers were pretty much at the mercy of their bosses. Workers were paid low wages, worked long hours, and had no benefits. Working conditions were often terrible. Child labor was common. And if you didn't like it you could quit because someone else was right behind you to take your job.

Then workers began to organize. Samuel Gompers

was one of the first leaders of the "Labor Movement." Workers demanded higher pay and better working conditions and said that if they didn't get them they would not work. *As a group, not as individuals,* they would "strike." They would throw up a picket line and keep any other workers from entering the factory. They would block delivery of raw materials. Needless to say, there was sabotage of factories that were struck and a lot of violence occurred. But a lot of businesses chose to deal with the *group* of workers, and they found it cheaper to pay a few more cents an hour than to close down. So "Organized Labor" got its start.

Over the years the unions gained strength, had victories, signed up more and more members, and "organized" more and more industries. Steel, coal, autos, communications, all became "organized."

As the unions became stronger, their weight was felt more and more in politics. When Roosevelt was elected in 1932, labor backed him and labor got paid. The National Labor Relations Act was passed creating a National Labor Relations Board to decide labor issues and labor's friends were appointed to that board.

By 1970, *about a third* of *all American workers were union members* and unions gave the biggest single block of money, of *any* group, to politicians' campaigns.

All a company had to do was agree to higher wages and then raise prices to pay for it. So most companies just agreed with unions and went about their business. No big deal. And the unions set up pension funds that became the target of schemes by organized crime, who had lent muscle to labor leaders in the past. The old friends of the labor leaders called their notes. And the unions became undemocratic. Union bosses treated their unions like *their* private property, they appointed relatives to cushie jobs, controlled elections to union office, paid themselves enormous salaries, and did little to earn those salaries. And the union membership began to fall. Competition from imported products cut into business's ability to give raises and pass it along in the form of higher prices. So the unions *couldn't deliver*. Unions lost more and more organizing elections.

When Ronald Reagan won the 1980 election, he appointed anti-labor people to the National Labor Relations Board. And in 1982 the air traffic controllers, a union of government workers, struck for higher wages and closed down the airports. Their strike was *illegal* and Reagan did the unthought of: He didn't knuckle down. He fired the air traffic controllers and replaced them with nonunion workers. That literally broke the back of organized labor. In addition, Reagan prosecuted many labor leaders for corruption and put them in jail. Labor union membership dropped to about 17% of all U.S. workers.

Today the only unions that are growing are government worker unions (i.e., the Teachers Union). More and more companies are nonunion, particularly in high-tech fields.

So there is a thumbnail history of the labor movement in the U.S. Now let's talk about concepts, *the theology of Labor and the left:*

"*Collective Bargaining.*" . . . The basic notion of organized labor is that *all workers are alike*. Therefore they bargain together and all get the same pay. The *worst worker* gets the same as the *best worker*. They rise and fall together. So why should anyone in a union job try harder? *They have nothing to gain!!!* Pay raises come with *seniority, not better work*. So why work harder? Sooner or later the unionized company will be beaten out by the nonunion company, where individual effort counts and job security comes with performance, *not* seniority!! . . . Think of how detrimental to a human being it must be to be nothing but the *average* of all your fellow workers. How dehumanizing it must be to know that your individual performance means *nothing!!* But that's the system in a union shop.

"*Class Solidarity.*" . . . Back in the 19th century a political school of thought developed that held that all of politics and economics was based on *class warfare* (rich against poor, bosses against employees, landlords against tenants, etc.). Marx and Lenin were adherents of that school and it is the basis of Communism (i.e., class "struggle"). They believed (and still do) that there is no mobility between classes, that the poor can never raise themselves up, that the rich will always keep the poor down. Therefore the poor, tenants and employees, must stick together (i.e., "class solidarity"). They even wrote an anthem called "Solidarity Forever." They refer to each other as "brother" . . . and that mentality *still* is the basis for unionism and that rhetoric pervades the union movement. Union members are always discouraged from any cooperation with management. Union members are always told that the only reason they ever get a raise is due to the efforts of the union leadership "collectively bargaining" at the "bargaining table." You hear this rhetoric all the time.

In fact, the union bosses are more repressive and anti-democratic than any capitalist "boss" could ever be. The union bosses retain power by dividing people and sowing discontent. They live like parasites on the blood of the workers as no manager would think of doing.

"Closed Shop" and *"Right to Work."* . . . The linchpin of organized labor is the organizing election. The union organizers target a company, try to find some discontented workers to spread rumors and trouble, then they call for an election. Under federal law if 51% of the workers vote to join the union, *all the workers have to pay dues* and the union is the "bargaining agent" for *all workers* even though 49% don't want to be union members. Then any new worker has to join the union. That's called a "closed shop." Some states have passed "Right to Work" laws. Those laws say that you don't have to join the union to be hired, only if you want to. That is anathema to the unions. It breaks their back. If you didn't have to pay union dues, would you? It cuts the union income drastically!

"AFL-CIO" . . . *Teamsters* . . . *UAW* . . . *"Locals."* . . . The American Federation of Labor (AFL) is a conglomerate of unions that merged with the Congress of Industrial Organizations (CIO) in the late '30s or early '40s to become the AFL-CIO, the largest labor organization in the world. The AFL-CIO threw the Teamsters Union out in the '50s due to corruption in the Teamsters Union. The United Auto Workers used to be the biggest single union of the AFL-CIO. I think the Teach-

ers Union is bigger now. . . . Theoretically all the "International" unions are associations of "Locals." The idea is that it's a "bottom up" deal. Wrong! It's a "top down" organization that has used mafia thugs for clout and now uses political contributions.

"*Scab.*" . . . In the union vernacular a "scab" is a nonunion worker that takes the place of a union member on strike. There is nothing worse to a union person than a strike-breaker.

You see "Proud to Be a Union Member" bumper strips. They are on the cars of the really hard-core unionists. Some people, that have such low self-esteem that they think their only hope is within a union, believe in the union like a religion. They blindly follow the union leadership, vote the union line, and preach the union gospel. . . . God help them!!

So now as you observe strikes or hear union rhetoric, you'll have a better understanding.

Love

Dad

3/18/94

Dear Jack,

We've talked about the various experiences one should have, in addition to a formal education, that will make for an "educated man." Some are: the Las Vegas experience of flash, glitz, fast money, thick makeup, and show; the commodities mart in Chicago where rumors are currency and millions can be made or lost in a span of minutes; the New York experience and all that it means; and the Washington, D.C., experience for all that it too means.

You've been introduced to the Vegas experience through Jeff, or at least a part of it.

I want to tell you a little about the New York experience in this letter and the Washington experience in one of my next letters.

New York City. The Big Apple. The crossroads of the world. . . . What is it really?

New York City is really five boroughs: Staten Island, Brooklyn, Queens, Manhattan, and the Bronx. But when people say "New York" they mean *Manhattan Island*.

New York is the center of the "Bos-Wash Corridor," meaning the solid sprawl of urbanized land that extends from Boston to Washington and includes Connecticut, New Jersey, eastern Pennsylvania, Rhode Island, Delaware, eastern Maryland, and the Washington suburbs of Virginia.

New York proper is the largest media market in the United States with over 10% of the U.S. population within 60 miles of Manhattan (25m people).

But New York is *much more than that*. It is the *Financial*

Center of the World (only recently being challenged *sometimes* by Tokyo and London). N.Y. has the stock market (Wall Street) and all that that includes (the headquarters of all the banks, investment banking firms, brokerage firms, etc.) . . . It is the Cultural Capital of the Western World. It has Broadway (plays and musicals), the networks' (ABC, CBS, & NBC) headquarters, the great publishing houses of books and magazines. It has the great art exhibitions and musicians of America. And more than that, it houses the cultural elite of America (the writers, columnists, and editors, the newscasters and celebrities).

It is the corporate capital of America. Most of the major U.S. companies are headquartered in New York. It's where the *big decisions are made*. Though Los Angeles has become the entertainment capital of the world (movies, records, etc.) a lot of entertainment industry decisions are still made in New York due to the networks, publishing, and financing that are in N.Y.

N.Y. is the Fashion Capital of the World (long ago it supplanted Paris) and though yarn and fabric are made in the South and a lot of cheap clothes are made in the Orient, N.Y. still makes most fashion clothing for America. . . . N.Y. is the center of education in America. There are more colleges and universities within 50 miles of N.Y. than I could name (Yale, Princeton, Columbia, NYU, West Point, University of Penn., Wharton, etc., are *just a few*). . . . Most of America's foundations are headquartered in N.Y. (Rockefeller, Ford, Carnegie, etc.).

With all of this, New York City is the *brain* & influence capital of the world.

. . . Oh yes, I forgot the U.N. The fact that the U.N. is in New York makes it the *Diplomatic Capital* of the World.

New York City *is really about money* . . . who *has it*, who *wants it*, and who *gets it*.

New York is a wild place. There are *few middle class in NYC* (they live out in the boroughs and in the suburbs and commute into the city to work). There is mostly the very rich, the very poor (Harlem is the north end of Manhattan Island), the tourists, the hustlers, and crooks. New York City is alive 24 hours a day. Restaurants and bars *don't close*. You can get any type of dinner and take in a show anywhere in Manhattan at 4:30 A.M.!!! There are stores open on many blocks 24 hrs. a day . . . New York City is *ethnic*. It seems like everyone but the elite are ethnic and speak with an accent. Over 200 different languages are spoken in NYC and *every* ethnic food has a restaurant (and usually a good one) every other block.
. . . NYC is *dirty*. The soot and grime is everywhere. You blow your nose and it's *black*. UGH! . . . NYC is dangerous. You will see someone being mugged as you ride by in a cab. Robberies take place in fine hotels. And people don't think a thing about it. NYC is *crowded, crowded, crowded*. You can't believe the mobs of people everywhere. . . . NYC is *expensive*. Expect to pay *double* for anything from a hot dog to parking (if you can find a place). But then, you don't drive in NYC (it's too expensive, and too dangerous, and too inconvenient). You take a cab or a limo or, if you can't afford that, the subway. On the streets all there are are cabs and limousines. . . . New Yorkers are rude. New Yorkers *ain't friendly*. It's the culture. It's dog eat dog. There is something going on all

the time in NY: plays, musicals, shows, lectures, exhibits, etc., etc.

New York *faces east*. Most of the people came from Europe and relate to Europe. The elite think nothing of going to Paris for the weekend (or London or Brussels). New Yorkers think NYC is the center of the earth and they think there are nothing but cowboys and sagebrush 50 miles west. They think westerners are dull and all "Valley Girl" types. They think the South is all "red-necks" and the West is another planet. Anything in between Los Angeles and New York is "fly-over" country. They "know" it all happens in NYC so why the hell should they care about anywhere else?

Because *New York is so influential*, because *New York has so much of the money*, because *so much happens in New York, you need the New York experience*. You need to *live there* and suck it all in. You need to be *familiar with it* and *be comfortable in it*.

A westerner who hasn't had the New York experience *really isn't an educated man.* . . . So *one day you'll do New York!!*

Love

Dad

3/22/94

Dear Jack,

I've written you about some of the experiences, besides formal education, that make for an "educated man." I wrote you about the "New York Experience." Now let's talk about the "Washington Experience."

I took you to Washington several years ago. You visited the capital, you met senators and congressmen. You visited the White House. You went to Arlington, the Smithsonian, Georgetown, and you climbed the Washington Monument. We visited the Vietnam Memorial and the Lincoln Memorial. You went to a dinner with Pat Buchanan, Wm. F. Buckley, Ollie North, and Gen. Singlaub. You met Jim Lake. . . . *That was just the surface of Washington, D.C.*

Washington is about POWER and Influence!! Washington is about who can get things done *in the world. Washington is the center of power in the world.* And as government has become more and more important and pervasive, Washington has become more and more important.

First of all, the majority of the population is black. They drive the cabs, they are the clerks in the government offices, the cops, the sanitation workers. But even though they run the city government, by and large, they are not the people who really run things in D.C.

There are 100 senators and 435 congressmen. *The ones with seniority*, who chair the committees and subcommittees of Congress, *have power*. You met Senator

Sam Nunn. *He has power.* The senior staff members of the senior legislators (Senate & House) *have power.*

The senior officials of the administration *have power.* The president, his senior staff, and his cabinet members *have power.*

The top lobbyists *have power.* There are lawyers who represent clients and nonlawyer lobbyists (like Jim) who raise money from their clients and contribute it to the campaign coffers of the legislators and, in exchange, get laws favorable to their clients passed by the Congress.

And there is the permanent establishment of Washington. They are the socialites, the newsmen, the columnists (like George Will), who grease the wheels of Washington. They can get a phone call taken, they can get a dinner invitation accepted, they have their opinion listened to.

And then there is the vast army of bureaucrats who do the "business" of government. They write regulations, publish data, design forms, and otherwise do things that *they think* are important and they try to convince everyone else that what they do is important. *Every day the Washington bureaucracy costs us $60,000,000* and *that's a single day's payroll. Every day!!!*

And then there are the visitors to Washington (not the sightseers, *the visitors*). They come from all over the country to get a government contract or bitch about an arbitrary regulation or plea for a law to be passed. They hire the lobbyists, they visit the congressmen, and they testify at the hearings.

And there are the "think tanks" (research groups for special interests) and the associations. It seems like every silly ass little group has an association with an office in Washington and a paid staff whose main job seems to be to convince them that their association is saving them from terrible troubles or getting them big favors. My brother is head of an association. Usually the heads of associations are former congressmen or senior staffers who join or set up the association to give themselves a job (Nixon's former press secretary is head of the truck stop owners association).

Everyone is jockeying for power or the *appearance of power*. Who can get in or get invited or get a bill passed or get a story played on national T.V. or an article written in a national magazine.

The catchword in Washington is "access." Can you get your phone call returned? Can you get in to see the man you want to see? The ultimate in "access" is to play golf with the president . . . *that's "access."* Lunch with a committee chairman is *"access" big time*. To be seen at that golf game or lunch is to let Washington know you have "access."

Again, to be an "educated man" you need to know your way around Washington, D.C. And to know your way around you need to have the "Washington Experience." If you do a summer internship for someone important or if you take a temporary staff job you'll get the "Washington Experience." If you work on a presidential campaign and are in and out of D.C. you can get the experience.

A lot of men (like Jim) went to D.C. to take a temporary staff slot and stayed. A lot of congressmen that lose elections back home stay in D.C. as lobbyists. . . . Power is seductive. Once some men are around it or have it, they have a hell of a time leaving it.

So the name of the game is "learn it and *leave it*." Washington is not a "real world." Power comes and goes. You have it one day and the next day it's gone. And seeing that is also part of the "Washington Experience."

So, one day, do it.

Love

Dad

4/10/94

Dear Jack,

Read this letter twice, then *photocopy it*. Put the photocopy in a place where you will be reminded to reread it each week until you graduate from Cate. Then photocopy it again and *read it every month through college*. With your ambition and desire to succeed, what you will by then have indelibly printed in your mind will help you achieve your desires.

The Harvard Business School recently did a study to determine the common characteristics of the top producers in the business world. This is what they found:

1. *They did not take "no" or rejection personally.* They have high self-esteem. They get disappointed, but they don't get devastated by setbacks.
2. *They take 100% responsibility for their results.* They don't blame others or circumstances. In fact, the worse the circumstances, the harder they work.
3. *They have high ambitions and a high desire to succeed.* And they set their priorities accordingly.
4. *They have high levels of empathy.* They put themselves in the other guy's shoes and anticipate the needs and desires of others.
5. *They are internally self-oriented.* They know where they are going, know how far along the way they are at any given time, and don't allow themselves to be sidetracked.
6. *They have high levels of willpower and determina-*

tion. They have self-discipline and they don't give up.

7. *They are impeccably honest.* No matter the temptation to fudge, they don't. So they are trusted by everyone.
8. *They have the ability to approach people.* Even when it is uncomfortable, they communicate to individuals and groups.
9. *They give attention to detail.*
10. *They know their business.*

Well, old boy, there you have it!! . . . A *blueprint for success*!!! Some people are born with those qualities. Most people have to develop them to one degree or another in themselves. In either case, the guys who have them succeed!! In spades!!

I've enclosed a rather interesting article from the paper. *The story is* that the best estimates were that it would take *9–12 months to repair I-10* after the January 17th quake. It was costing an estimated $2 million a day in wasted commute time and extra gas. *So,* Governor Wilson used his emergency powers to cut the normal bullshit and government red tape and he unleashed private contractors and gave them an incentive to beat a "hurry up" target of June 24th. Then Wilson kicked ass to insure that the bureaucrats didn't screw things up. . . . VOILA!!! . . . The project was completed in just *84 days, 74 days* before the target date.

And now the Democrats give no credit to private enterprises or to Wilson. They complain that the contractor "made money.". . . I can't believe it! Oh yes I do!!

One Democrat said, "See what government can do when it wants to." Asshole, government had not a thing to do with it except get out of the way.

It was that Wilson was facing an election year and needed a feather in his cap. . . . He got one!

But most of all it shows that American private business is the best in the world and American businessmen can *really deliver*. Just get the parasites of government out of the way. Let the profit motive work. And the Democrats hate it!! Those bastards have been destroying our country for 50 years, sucking its blood for the special interests they represent.

Perhaps the lesson of free enterprise and political will won't be lost on the public (or at least that part that doesn't work for the government).

I'm looking forward to seeing you Parents' Weekend. . . . Just 10 days off!!

    Love

        Dad

SENIOR
YEAR

9/9/94

Dear Jack,

When I got home from Cate Monday afternoon I pulled the photo album from 1991 to look at the pictures of that day I left you three years ago at Savage House. I didn't know whether to *laugh* or *cry*. You have grown so much from the day I left a little fourteen-year-old freshman on "the Mesa." You were five feet tall, so enthusiastic yet so scared, never had been abroad, never had held a job in your life, and were almost *sweet! How life has changed.*

Well, you're now a senior, almost 18, a big man on campus (BMOC), and you only have 25% of your Cate career to go. You can look back at your previous three years with a lot of pride. You don't have straight A's, but your grades are pretty damn good and I really believe you have done about as well as you could.

You ain't Student Body President of Cate. *You* chose *not* to be. You *could have been*, but *you chose not* to do it. I think that was a big mistake, but again, it was *your* choice. You ain't a prefect. I think you got screwed on that one. You and I both know you deserved that, and the fact you ain't a prefect is plain *unfair*. But Jack, you learned a great lesson: *Life isn't always fair.* You don't always get what you deserve and sometimes you don't deserve what you *do get* (both good and bad). And you'll have to ask yourself why you ain't a little closer to some really nice guys (like Butterworth). I suspect that you don't really *put yourself out* much to some people. You'll have to ask yourself why you don't. If you got out of yourself a bit more and extended more friendship and sincere concern to more people, you would have many more good friends.

But, on balance, you have reached the ¾ point in pretty good shape.

So, with 25% of your "Cate Career" left, just 8 *months*, what should your priorities be? Might I suggest:

1. Focus on academics. *Learn*. Keep your grades up. Don't let down and hurt your GPA. Get the very best Cate has to offer. Spend some *private time* with some of your teachers. Ask probing questions. Be *reflective* and *intellectually curious*.

2. Maintain your values. Seniors have more latitude, more freedom. Don't abuse it or flaunt it. Again, *use common sense* and *do what's right* (that also means *don't* do what's *wrong*).

3. *Reach out* to more people. Be sensitive to where other people are coming from. Every day, that's *every day*, try to do something *kind* to *someone*. If you see someone hurting, put your arm on their shoulder. If you see one of the less popular people walking alone, say "Hi."

4. Be a *leader*. That means positive *and* negative: "We ought to do . . ." "Let's . . ." as well as, "Let's not . . ." "We don't want to . . . do we." That means, "*You* can . . ." and "*We* can . . ." *Encourage people!!*

5. *Have FUN*. Enjoy this last year "on the Mesa."

Jack, I'm very proud of you. You have grown so much these past three years, *inside* and *outside*. I gave you that Kipling poem on your 12th birthday. It ends with the words, "Yours is the earth and everything that's in it, and—which is more—*You'll be a Man, my son.*"

Well, it's six years later and *you are a man, my son.*

    Love

Dad

10/24/94

Dear Jack,

I enjoyed "Parents' Weekend" a lot, even though I had only two days, not the usual three. You looked great and generally seemed to have your act together.

You obviously have a problem with expository writing. It comes out in exams and letters, etc. As the problem recurs, it is compounded by a growing mental block. . . . You need to do several things: (1) Take that writing "enrichment" course Cate offers. (2) Ask for some help with *technique* from last year's English teacher and your art history teacher. (3) Practice . . . and write me those *two*, 15-minute, letters a week as you promised (enclosed are the stamps you asked for). If you do those three things, I guarantee you it will help. Otherwise this impediment will hamper your progress for years to come.

If, as you said, you ceased to look forward to being with Beth; if it wasn't fun and was always heavy; and if it really wasn't worth it anymore; then I agree with your breaking it off. I only caution you to treat her gently. Don't rub another girl in her face! And always speak well of her and be nice to her.

One other issue comes to mind, Jack. Your ability (or *inability*) to deal with disputes or disagreements. You said you and I were "at war" for a couple of weeks. I disagree with that characterization. I had a serious problem with you, I stated it in a manner designed to get your attention and, hopefully, cause you to alter your behavior. . . . That's not "at war," that's love. Jack, I think people can disagree without being disagreeable. I think people, particularly people who love each other, can confront an issue, deal with it, then get back, *quickly*, to their normal relationship. Jack, you tend to avoid confrontation, blow off problems, and skirt issues. That can be *very* destructive!! When an issue isn't dealt with, *it remains, festers,* and *usually gets worse.* It's been my experience that the sooner an issue is confronted and dealt with (by agreement or some sort of compromise), the sooner it's past. And I believe that it's *healthy* to argue out issues, sometimes vehemently, and thus to resolve them. I think it's *unhealthy* to avoid issues, push them under the rug, and not deal with honest differences. You could build your skills in this area.

Jack, I guess the word for now is: FOCUS. You need to focus on your priorities, on your grades, on your college applications, and on correcting any deficiencies you have (i.e., communication).

I love you a lot, son. I'm sure you will do well.

Love

Dad

11/9/94

Dear Jack,

I can't tell you how crushed I am over the Roderick situation. His dad and I have become friends and I know he has been concerned about Roderick for several reasons, one being that he never wrote or called home. That's never a healthy sign. The fact that Roderick would flagrantly break a rule, six months before graduation, when he was on probation, was just plain *suicidal*, and that's *sick*!!

I can't imagine how his dad feels. The *shame, disappointment*, and *hurt* has to be *killing* him. I don't know what I can say to him other than to express my sorrow.

As for Roderick, the shame, not getting a Cate diploma after 3½ years and having that on his record (and don't think it isn't) to haunt him all his life at every job interview or security clearance, *I just can't believe he was so dumb*.

But Jack, learn from this. Learn that if you break the rules you pay the price. That's the flip side of "doing what's right": When you do what's wrong, you pay. It may seem harsh at times, but if it isn't so, the whole society suffers. That's one of the causes of so much crime in America.

Anyway, my heart goes out to Roderick and mostly to his dad.

Last night's election results went beyond my wildest hopes. Other than Jeb Bush in Florida and Ollie in Virginia and *maybe* Huffington, we won *every race* coast to coast. *Not one Republican incumbent lost*. So much for

Clinton, personally. His policies, and the Democratic party, were *thoroughly repudiated*. Clinton said he felt the voters' pain. Well, they made sure he did yesterday!! After the election he claimed his policies weren't repudiated. BS. He is lying again or just doesn't get it.

An interesting factoid is that a nation's humor reflects a great deal on its real character and soul. I've never heard *in my lifetime* the level of viciousness of the jokes aimed at a president as those about Clinton. . . . Those jokes and their popularity really foretold the election results.

I've enclosed a George Will article. *Please read it!!* I think you'll get a lot out of it.

That's it for now. Your word was "two 15-minute letters a week, I promise." . . . It's been three weeks *without one letter*. Jack, what is your word worth? Think about it.

Love

Dad

11/15/94

Dear Jack,

We've talked about college before, but let's have another go at it.

Some kids know exactly what they want to be in life, some don't. For those who do, college is a trade school. Whether they want to be a doctor, lawyer, teacher, psychologist, chemist, engineer, or whatever, they take the required courses for a degree in that subject and whatever "electives" catch their fancy. They get their degree and they are on their way. Usually they have met other kids in their field of study that they will run into later in their career, but that's incidental.

Most kids, and you are in this group, have a general idea of their interests and ability, but don't really know exactly where they want to end up.

So . . . how to pick the right college and how to structure your course of studies. A lot of kids don't really have much of a choice. Money or their grades pretty much dictate where they will go to school and when they get there, course availability dictates what they will take. You have the grades from a prestigious school and a father willing to back you, so you, fortunately, have a choice.

So, what's my recommendation and why?

First, the college.

If you want to live in the West and do business on the Pacific Rim, then go to a western college. We've already talked about why.

You should pick a college based on several criteria:

A. Is it a place you want to spend four years of your life?. . . Both LA (USC or UCLA) or the Peninsula (Stanford) are great. They both are cultural centers, have a great social life, the weather is great, etc., etc., etc. The weather is shitty in some areas, some colleges are in podunk towns where they roll up the streets at 9:00 P.M.

B. What kind of kids go there and are they the type you want to associate with for four years, and know for the rest of your life?. . . Some colleges have a group of pretty average types, OK, but certainly not very special. The smaller colleges (i.e., Reed, Claremont, etc.) draw a certain type of person. The prestigious colleges (i.e., Harvard, Princeton, Yale, Stanford, etc.) draw the cream of the crop, the top 1%, intellectually and on other bases. Some have the social skills, many don't. Certainly the top 1% stays the top 1% as they move into politics, business, and the professions. And their relationships with old college chums sure doesn't hurt. USC, Ohio State, Michigan State, the University of Texas, LSU, Auburn, Vanderbilt, etc., the "second tier" schools, are not quite as good as the most prestigious schools, but plenty good enough.

C. What's in a name? "Cate," "Thacher," "Andover," "Choate," "Harvard," "Stanford," "Princeton," "Yale," and yes, "USC"? It sure turns a head, gets you in the door, and *means something*. Now then, are successful men successful because they went to great schools and got a great education, or were they great guys, which would have made them successful anyway and that's what got them into the top schools in the first place?

Now let's look at why *you* are going to college (not in order).

1. To have fun, meet friends you'll have all your life, and mature.

2. To become an "educated man." You will learn about many things by taking courses in many subjects. You will attend seminars, go to lectures and hear great speakers. Your mind will grow and you will sharpen your intellect. In the process you will gravitate toward certain fields of study that will suggest a career path. As this happens, you will choose a "major" in that field, focus your energy in that direction, and become better prepared for a career in whatever field. Then graduate school becomes your "trade school" in business, finance, law, etc.

Jack, I got the best part of my education at Oakland City College because I *thirsted* for knowledge, wanted to learn, *really learn*, and put out a hell of a lot of effort. OCC sure wasn't a great school, but I was a *strong student*. Conversely, you can blow through a great school, just get the grades but not really become educated. It's not likely but it's possible. So just because a USC isn't a Harvard, *it's really you who will determine what you get out of your education*.

So, what's all this mean? Bottom line is: Get into a

Stanford or a Harvard if you can, USC or UCLA if you can't. Then throw yourself into *learning*, sucking up the academic environment and spirit of education. Get the most out of the 4 years, because you'll only be there once. Meet as many people as you can. Be a friend, make friends, network, and do some extracurricular activities.

Jack, you're on the right path to success and happiness. You'll do well at Stanford or USC or UCLA. It's really up to you in college as it has been at Cate. Your Cate education was as much a function of Jack as it was of Cate.

Ken has been coming by fairly frequently. He thinks the world of you and asks about you each time I see him.

I'm working my ass off. Things are going well but not fast enough for my liking. I guess I'll just have to work harder.

Love

Dad

1/4/95

Dear Jack,

After day-to-day crisis, perhaps the most vexing thing in a teenager's life is the question of, "What am I going to be?" and "Where am I really going?" The problem is that you can never really know where you're going and *what it will be like*, until you get there. But then, if you can't know where you're going, how do you have direction or really prepare yourself? How can you know that what you are doing, on a day-to-day basis, is going to help you later on?

We've talked about this before but let's revisit the issue and address a couple of basic principles:

Most kids think of their future in terms of what they "want to be." People always ask them, "What do you want to be when you grow up?" A lot of kids say they want to be a lawyer without knowing what a lawyer *does* or what it takes to *be* a lawyer, or a "doctor," without knowing what it takes to become a doctor or what a doctor really *does* (like being "on call" nights and weekends, and being interrupted during dinner parties, or movies, to go to an emergency).

The real problem is that it is so difficult to really know what kind of life a particular career entails unless you're *doing it*. And by then it's too late!! The die is cast. Even if your father is a doctor, and you live with him, the life of a doctor (or engineer, or lawyer, or teacher) is very likely to change radically by the time *you* become one.

Volkswagen used to have an ad titled: "A *thing is what it does.*" Well, so is a man.

The real issue isn't what you want to be, but *what you want to do.*

Steven Spielberg was making movies when he was eight years old. He loved it. It wasn't a matter of money, or title, or position, or prestige, he just *liked to make movies.* So he became good at it. Or maybe he was good at it because he liked it. And because he was so good, he made millions!

On the other hand, David Gauvin always wanted to *be* a doctor. When he finally became one, he *hated it.* He used to tell me he hated putting his head "between those smelly feet." What he really loved was his real estate investments. So, after all that work in medicine, and with no business, finance, or real estate training, he went into real estate (and got into trouble).

You watched the interview with Peter Robinson, the author (of *Snapshots from Hell: The Making of an* MBA, the Stanford business school book), the other day. There was a young man that went from position to position within the academic world, each time doing a terrific job at what he was doing. Opportunities kept presenting themselves and he kept meeting people that did him some good. By the time he was in his mid-thirties he was doing exactly what he wanted and making excellent money doing it.

So Jack, what's the answer for *you?*

First, you want to be an *educated, capable* man. You want to be *qualified* to exploit opportunities as they arise. Do get a good education! Take a *variety* of course studies (i.e., take a lot of "survey of _____" courses;

those are the introductions and overviews of sociology, psychology, geology, business, English, literature, etc., etc., etc.).

Second, as you get your education, associate with as many people as you can (don't always hang with one clique), travel as much as you can, and involve yourself in as many situations as you can. That way you'll learn the most about your abilities and your likes and dislikes. You will also get exposure to the maximum contacts for your future.

Third, remember and realize that you can be just about *anything* you want to be. You have the brains, personality, looks, and health to have your pick. Not everyone is so lucky. So choose carefully. Don't exclude anything, don't let preconceptions guide you away from any possibility.

Fourth, have the confidence that *it's only going to get better*. The more you learn, the more people you meet, the more places you go, the more people you'll meet, places you will go, and the more you'll learn. As your horizons broaden you will have more and more and better and better choices. And that's a good life.

Fifth, realize that it's not just the destination that counts but also the journey. I've seen people say, "I hated college and I hate my job, but when I retire I'll have a great life." Then they die a year after they retire . . . a wasted life, for what? So enjoy it step by step and gain satisfactions each step of the way.

Jack, you're doing great and you will do great. Enjoy it and don't worry. It will all happen if you work at it.

Dad

1/5/95

Dear Jack,

I thought I might start the new year by sharing a bunch of random concepts with you. These are ideas, observations, or "Rules of Life" that come from my experience. Some are rather obvious, some not so obvious.

1. Military service (Cameron), a major accident (your dad), a nasty divorce, a major illness, all are *seminal events* in a lifetime. When these events occur, they *take over a life*, become an *obsession*, and literally you can bracket a period of *years* that it will take before a person's life and *independent judgment* return to normal. When dealing with people in this cycle, keep in mind what is preoccupying them.

2. *Thoughtfulness builds friendship.* That call or note of sympathy or congratulations, that invitation for a drink . . . *they count.* Remembering a birthday or anniversary or kid's name . . . *counts.* If you want to have a friend . . . *be a friend.* And remember that it *counts triple* when someone is *down*, because *everyone* is his friend when he is up.

3. Einstein discovered (invented) the space/time continuum. There is also a physical/mental health continuum. If you are mentally unhealthy, you will get *physically* sick. If you are physically ill, it will drastically affect you mentally. The question is what comes first, the chicken or the egg. And how do you break a down cycle: If

you're down mentally how do you get *up* before you get sick (or throw your back out) and if you are sick how do you keep your spirits up. Just recognizing that this powerful correlation exists will help a lot.

4. Most people fall into (or join) a "subculture." Remember that the word *"cult"* comes from *"culture."* These subcultures can be a religious affiliation, a civic group (i.e., Rotary), drugs, a hobby, union membership, gambling, a sports activity, etc. Frequently, that subculture becomes so *consuming* that it *overshadows* family, job, and friends, and affects judgments on unrelated issues. . . . So look for the subculture.

5. A person's self-image usually establishes the arena in which he plays, much more than his *real ability*. There are a lot of city councilmen who could be congressmen, but they *set their sights low*. There are a lot of small businessmen who have more ability than *big* businessmen, but they *don't think* they can play a bigger game. Frequently, all it takes to be a "world class" player is to *get into* a "world class" arena and *play by "world class" rules*. I once asked a major player what the difference was in his world. He said "it's just 'aughts' (meaning zeroes) . . . meaning that it's the *same game* just played with *more zeros*. So *you* have to decide whether you want to be a "world class" player and deal with more zeros (and more expensive—i.e., beautiful—cars and women). . . . *It's up to you*.

6. The Bible says, "There is a time for reaping and a

time for sowing." The song says, "You got to know when to hold 'em and know when to fold 'em." The point is that *you buck the trends at your peril.* I've started a business right at the start of a recession and had to work like hell for meager results, where if I had *timed* it better, I would have done much better with a hell of a lot less work. They say *"timing is everything"* and *they're right.*

7. People who are *comfortable* with themselves . . . boy, can you tell!! They are the men who *like* being men and the women who *like* being women. They are the men who exude confidence, don't *try too hard*, don't try to be *something they ain't.* They give the impression that *if they like themselves you should, too.* And boy, can you spot a person who isn't at peace with himself.

8. Your *roots.* What are you moored to? Some people are Catholic, Methodist, or Baptist. Some are Irish, Italian, or English. Some are middle-class or upper-class. Some are American or Japanese or Mexican. When you meet a man you need to look at *what are his roots?* It will tell you a lot about that man and how to relate to him. If he is a Jew, he will be different than an Irish Catholic. Some people really have no "roots" and it shows. . . . What are your "roots," Jack?

9. "Causes." Boy, can some people get caught up in a "cause" (i.e., anti-abortion, women's rights, anti-war or anti-nuclear weapons, etc., etc.). It really seems that causes are *almost a narcotic* to some people: It gets their juices flowing, it gives

greater *meaning* to their lives, it makes them feel *important*, it gives them instant friends. It sometimes seems that the more screwed up a person's life is, the more they need a "cause" and are susceptible to falling into one. That is not to say that getting involved "*temporarily*" in a great cause isn't worthy and isn't worthwhile. It's to say that a man needs to look at whether *the cause* or *personal need for a cause* is the real motivation. It's *really tough* to argue a cause with a person who personally *really needs that cause* to give meaning to his life.

Well, Jack, those are just some random thoughts you might keep in mind as you go through life.

Enclosed is a copy of Scott's recommendation letter. Jack, you have to be *really proud of yourself* to have *earned* such a letter. *I'm* proud of you. You really need to send a thank-you note to Scott.

Jack, these last holidays were about as nice for your old dad as he can remember. Your company was a joy. I was touched by your generosity to others. That's really what the spirit of Christmas is all about. Jan *really* appreciated your gift. . . . It meant so much to her.

See you soon.

Love

Dad

1/11/95

Dear Jack,

This is another of those "how to" letters for you to put in your *Instruction Manual of Life*. I guess that it's not the highest priority in your life today, but I thought that it's not too early to plant some seed in your mind.

The question is, "Who do you need in life?" I suggest that there is a whole group of people that you need a special relationship with, so that your needs will be fulfilled in the manner that *you* desire, as various situations arise. I further suggest that a successful man will *cultivate* these relationships, some long before the need arises, so that, *when needed,* the *right* person is there and will perform in a *highly motivated* manner.

There is a basic list and then a rather exotic list.

The basic list:

1. A first-rate tax accountant. . . . I've been with Swanton for 20 years.
2. A first-rate business operations accountant . . . Steve Richards has been my friend for over 12 years.
3. A good general business lawyer. . . . Bob Hillison has been my friend for 15 years.
4. A good barber. . . . I've been going to Lonnie for 20 years.
5. A good firewood source. . . . I've been getting my wood from Gilbert for 10 years.

6. A first-rate internal medicine doctor. . . . I've been going to Dr. Uhrle for 10 years.
7. A first-rate dentist. . . . I've been going to Dr. Benneyan for 20 years.
8. A first-rate stockbroker & commodities trader. . . . I *recently* found Chris. For the past several years I haven't been trading stocks or commodities.
9. A first-rate *local* banker. . . . You need a local "relationship" for the personal service that a local bank can render if they like you and trust you. I've been with USB for years, they are unbelievably great! George and Dennis are real pros.
10. A first-rate "money center" bank relationship (i.e., Wells, B of A, Citibank, etc.). The larger banks perform international and interstate services and have much larger lending limits.
11. A good travel agent.
12. A very competent general insurance agent.

There is your basic list. These are the people you deal with on a regular basis and boy can they make your life easier if they are on your team. You have to refer clients to them, shoot straight in your dealings with them, inquire about their families, and even socialize with them. And boy does it make a difference!!

Now then, the more exotic list. This is the list if you really want to be a "player" and a "connected man":

1. You need to have a friend at the local newspaper. You can get a story in the paper or get a story "softened" that is going in the paper. You can get "tipped" on stories that are about to break. You can check people out. But, you need to feed stuff that's happening. You'd be surprised what a local newspaper contact can do for you.

2. You need a contact with the local police department. You'd be surprised at the favors & information you can get.

3. You need friends in local government (i.e., city councilmen, mayors, county supervisors). You make a friend by being a friend (i.e., help with campaign, contribute a little money, attend a function).

4. You need friends in state and national government. Again, same rules apply as to local government. It helps when you know your congressmen, assemblymen, etc. And you'd be surprised at all they can do for you.

5. You need contacts at destination resorts, amusement parks, etc. (i.e., Universal Studios, Mirage, Yosemite, etc.). It's always nice to get your friends or family in and get VIP treatment. Again, make a friend by being a friend. There is always some issue they need support on or assistance with. And you can call on your friends in government or the news media to help. . . . See how it all interrelates!!!

I suggest that you commit yourself to being "a player." Get involved, make friends by being a friend, and enjoy the fruits of "having influence." At the very least your life will be easier and more pleasant. Sometimes you'll have a real need and a friend will come through.

Do it.

     Love

          Dad

1/23/95

Dear Jack,

What a great day Saturday! The drive to Cate was beautiful with the air so clean and the magnificent snow over Tejon Pass. Lunch was great and we had a chance to visit with the Bonnings. Then the game: Your first goal blew me away! You know, after three years I still don't really understand the subtleties of lacrosse. Then Steph's birthday dinner w/ Jeff, Davis, & Anna. It brought back memories of when you and Steph were so little. . . . Anyway, great day!!

There is an old saying that "the exception makes the rule." I don't really know about that, but I do know that some people you and I have known (some just I) are proof positive of some of the rules of life:

1. *When you're down you can go up and when you're up you can go down.* Look at President Bush with a 92% approval rating one year before the election . . . then he lost. Look at Governor Wilson with a 19% approval a year before his election . . . a year later he beat the "can't lose," odds-on favorite. . . . Corollary: *Anticipate change!!*

2. *A man whose sole goal in life is money can end up a pretty miserable person even if he achieves great wealth.* John Garabedian started out as a poor immigrant Armenian fruit picker with only a high school education. He worked 18 hours a day, schemed, ran roughshod over everyone, bribed

politicians, and all he wanted was more & more money. He once told me he "didn't want friends because sooner or later a friend wants something." He died alone, but for his dogs, in a tiny house on one of his ranches. He had never traveled outside California. He died a despised man without a friend in the world. There was no funeral because nobody would have come. He had no children and his wife had died ten years before him. He was worth perhaps $200 million when he died.

3. *Hubris can cause a man a great fall.* Exactly a year ago Art was a pillar of the community, the president of a company, married, with a daughter, and happy as a pig in mud. He thought he could do no wrong, had an affair with an employee, apparently shaved the corners in a transaction, and got caught all around. Today he is out of work and divorced. How the mighty can fall when they think they can't.

4. *Some people are just plain born and bred to the manor.* Carol is the daughter of a rich, successful surgeon. Her mother was very ambitious for herself and her daughter. Her daughter went to UCLA and married a doctor. . . . Could it have been otherwise?

5. *An otherwise great man can have immense personal flaws that cause his downfall.* Richard Nixon and his paranoia and lack of real self-confidence.

6. *A man can get locked into a job he hates, or that bores him, because the money is so good.* Cotter

hates his job at ABC, but he can't leave because it pays so much. So he wastes his life, miserable, big paycheck to big paycheck.

7. *An inheritance can be a millstone if it isn't enough to really matter.* Tony had just enough inherited money to attract a gold digger wife who made him miserable. He had just enough to make him think he had to keep up appearances. He had just enough to kill his personal ambition. But he didn't have enough to *really* be comfortable or enough to do anything important with.

8. *Don't believe things, no matter how stable they appear, can't change.* Frank spent 23 years with Union Oil, a company noted for its internal stability, worked his way up to president of a subsidiary, and appeared to be set for life. Internal politics, getting on the wrong side of the wrong people (the chairman), and Frank was forced out. And he hasn't been the same since.

9. *Some very gifted & blessed men piss it all away.* Steve Carr won medals, was elected to the state senate, and was a "golden boy." He started boozing and womanizing and ended up divorced and losing his senate seat!!

10. *Some men are just plain good, guileless, no secret agenda people.* Your grandfather worked his way through Stanford, worked his whole career for one company, had lunch with his wife almost every day, never played around, his only activity was tennis, and died at peace. So there.

11. *Some men work hard enough and achieve all their*

dreams. Jack Woolf is an honorable, hardworking, bright, principled man. All Jack wanted was to be secure, a farmer, and have his sons with him in business. He is on several boards, is on the board of trustees of a university, is universally respected, three of his four sons are with him on the ranch (the 4th, a dentist), and his two daughters are happily married. And he is worth a lot. And he started with very little. So there.

12. *Some men are always positive. They never let negatives get to them.* Richard Hill would see a problem and he would say, "Well, here's another opportunity." . . . He was a success.

13. *Interest compounds.* Little Al Connell, short, ugly, and with a withered arm and all, started off after WWII making auto loans. He let his interest compound and he retired a *very very* rich man.

Jack, there are a lot more rules of life. And there are a lot of men you know that are proof positive of their validity.

Observe life's scene. Develop your own rules of life. . . . And live with them. Be comfortable with yourself and *your* values. And know how you arrived at them.

Love

Dad

2/5/95

Dear Jack,

We've talked a lot about our country and how lucky we are to be citizens of the United States of America. We've talked about the American Constitution and the rights, unique in the world and unique in human history, that are yours just for being a citizen.

We've talked about the men who wrote our Constitution and all they sacrificed to found our country. And we've talked about the men who have fought and died to keep this country free.

They gave us the rights we now enjoy. And we keep hearing about more and more rights: gay rights, women's rights, minority rights, etc., etc., etc.

All right, what about the reciprocal responsibilities? Nothing in life is free, or at least ought not to be free.

Jack, you are a citizen of the United States of America, the State of California, the City of Fresno, and a member of our family. You have obligations to each and can expect reciprocal rights. You have duties and you have privileges.

Remember when you were a little boy and I told you you had duties around the house? (The trash cans, the toilets, dusting once a week, washing the car, etc.) Other kids got paid for chores, but I told you it was your *duty* as a member of our family, so you didn't get paid. Period. I told you you also had rights: food, electricity, etc. Those types of things were your right as a member of our family. Special stuff you had to earn or would be given to you just out of love.

Well, Jack, the same goes for your citizenship:

For your country, state, and city, you have basic responsibilities: to vote, to obey the laws, to perform jury duty, if requested, and to defend against aggression, with military service, if called upon.

If you consider yourself a really responsible citizen you should do even more than the basics: walk a precinct for a candidate of your choice, make a contribution to a candidate of your choice, serve on a board or commission, etc. At least be informed on public issues and communicate your opinions to elected officials.

The founding fathers envisioned that farmers, merchants, and professionals would also serve from time to time as elected officials. In recent years we have spawned a "politician class" that views government as a career and goes to all ends to feather that nest. Perhaps in the "age of Newt" and term limits, you will choose to serve for a time as an elected official. And perhaps you will be more highly thought of than the current "political class."

Perhaps as a citizen you will rally to a cause, such as teen gangs, thugs, graffiti, etc., and lead a public group to action.

Perhaps you will join a philanthropy board (such as the Art Museum) and help out with that cause. Perhaps you will join a service club, such as Rotary, or Kiwanis, and help with their activities in your community.

I know you will lead a family that has values and you will pass on your ideals to your children. You will be a good father and husband, and in that way be a contributing citizen of your community.

Remember when you were a little boy and I stopped a

police officer to introduce you and let you know he was your friend and you should always obey a policeman and call him if you needed help? That was being a good citizen and passing it on to my family. I'm sure you will do the same with your son. A little thing, but your responsibility.

Jack, you have all the rights and privileges of citizenship. Remember always that you also have duties as a citizen. You have responsibilities that go with the rights.

And then having fulfilled your responsibilities you can pass on the rights, intact, to the next generation.

In America, like ole "civus Romanus" in ancient Rome, we are citizens of a great land. Those who would tribalize us under the old play of "divide and conquer" must fail. We're not Black-American, Native-American, Hispanic-American. We're *American*. *Period*. We all have the same rights. And we all have the same responsibilities.

We've been balkanized with affirmative action, set-asides and other "special" rights for some people. I haven't seen a call for special responsibilities, other than the call for the rich to pay off special groups for their loyalty at the polls, and ignore lack of citizenship on the part of those same people. Those making that call do a great disservice to our country.

Jack, we will continue to be a strong nation if we *all* have our rights, respect, and fulfill the responsibilities of being a citizen.

That is America. Always be proud to be an American (boy, that ought to be a song).

Love

Dad

2/8/95

Dear Jack,

Your sister is so much fun I can't stand it. I picked her up at school yesterday for our every-other-Wednesday dinner and I flashed on how much she is like you were at her age (other than that she isn't very affectionate, but then she lives with her mother). She's quick, has a great sense of humor, and is totally cooperative. I'm not sure she realizes how much I look forward to my time with her. You know, in the seven years (God, it's been that long!!!) since the divorce, I have only missed one scheduled visit with her. She is growing up so much. Age 11 and already a young lady. And she likes sushi just like you did.

The fog is still socking in the valley. God is it miserable!! It was terrific to head up the grapevine Saturday, leave the fog and spend the day with you in sunshine. Coming down the grapevine on the way home Steph held her hand out the window, and as we dropped 4,000 feet in 10 minutes or so, the temperature dropped from 80 degrees to 45 degrees . . . that's a 35 degree differential!! Damn.

We really enjoyed your game. The team was a bit flat but that's usual after your win over Thacher, just three days before. And the Dunn team didn't pose that great a competition. Anyway, good game.

A friend of mine called me yesterday about a business problem. It raises a point that you ought to ponder: **When** do you fight and when do you compromise? The **age-old issue** of "Pragmatism or Principle."

In some cases, Jack, the issue is fairly straightforward: If someone owes you $3,000 and the legal fees to collect it are going to be $3,000 and it's going to take up your time and psychic energy, then you write it off. Consider it a lesson, learn from it, take your lumps, and move on. Some people say, "Pursue the bastard to his grave, don't let him get away with it, nobody screws me without a fight!!" I say forget it. It's not worth it.

OK, what if someone makes a claim against you that is pure bullshit? Let's say they claim $3,000 and you know it will cost $5,000 to defend. The arithmetic says pay it and save $2,000. The principle is, will you give in to fraudulent extortion? And if one guy can do it to you, then will there ever be an end? Businesses face this problem every day. People claim a store negligently left fruit on the floor that caused what's called a "slip and fall." Shyster lawyers file suit, claim damages, and the store knows it's cheaper to pay the lawyer off than fight the suit. But if they don't, there will be endless shyster lawyers right behind the first one. So they fight the case.

OK, what if some punk challenges you, embarrasses you in front of your lady, and wants to fight? He has nothing to lose, you do. . . . Drop it, leave, don't risk an injury for the principle of your "manhood." You risk injury or a scar or a broken tooth. For what? It's plain not worth it!!

I guess the real issue becomes, what principles are worth fighting for at what cost?

So, Jack, ponder this question. It's a serious one, and a man ought to have a philosophical framework in his mind as the issues arise.

That's about all for now.

Only three weeks to spring break so focus on your studies and go into your break confident that you're in good shape scholastically.

    Love

      Dad

2/16/95

Dear Jack,

You've been raised in a conservative, business-oriented, practical, middle-class home. You were not raised a member of the "noblesse oblige" class. Your father was not a member of a "caring profession" (i.e., social worker).

Words like "sincere," "compassion," "caring," "deprived," "underprivileged," "people of color," "physically challenged," "ACLU," "civil service," "diversity," and the like were not common currency in our home. We weren't "bleeding hearts."

You were taught "duty" and "responsibility" and "individualism."

I think I need to talk to you a bit about "compassion" and "sensitivity," not in the self-righteous, self-important way those words are so frequently used. And not in the self-aggrandizing sense that the bureaucrats use the words to justify their jobs and reach for ever bigger budgets. Those words, and others, have become shorthand for membership in the self-satisfied, holier-than-thou, liberal class of collectivists.

John Donne was a 17th century English poet and essayist. He wrote the famous lines, "No man is an island, entire of itself. . . . Any man's death diminishes me because I am involved in mankind. . . . Never send to know for whom the bell tolls, it tolls for thee."

The 17th and 18th centuries saw the rise of social liberalism as a reaction to the excesses of industrialization. Caring for "the poor" and "crippled" and "orphans" began to be thought of as a duty of the privileged upper classes. Therefore, if you "cared," you were associating yourself with the gentry. That tradition continues to this day and has become institutionalized in the welfare state.

It is no accident that Teddy Kennedy (rich, inheritor) "cares" and is liberal. As is Jay Rockefeller. As was Heinz etc., etc., etc. Add to them those whose livelihood depends on "caring" and you get a pretty big group of influential "carers."

But if they represent something you do not, then what ought you be?

First, you've been taught manners and to be sensitive to the feelings of those around you. You've been taught to have a sense of responsibility for those in your family, in your dorm, and in your school. Those are the basics of being a civilized man.

Now, you need to think about your sense of "feeling for others" and "compassion" in a broader way.

The Man of La Mancha sang about "fight the unbeatable foe" and "to fight for the right without question or pause." But I'm not advocating the impossible dream.

What I *am* advocating is that Jack Broome cultivate a real sense of compassion and feeling for the lives of those in your country, outside of the immediate circle of friends and acquaintances, and in the world.

You will realize that you really can't have much effect on those poor starving souls in Biafra. But your caring for their plight adds to your own humanity. And in some way you might be able to do some good you otherwise never would have, had you just plain not cared.

And if you use your good sense in these matters, it will give you a useful perspective.

I always remember the pastor at First Presbyterian telling about his trip to the starving people in Africa, and showing pictures of himself and five companions squatting down around a dying kid. Then he asked for donations to a fund for African missionaries. What he didn't say was that, at church expense, he and five big shots from the church went to Africa for one day, by way of New York (a day layover with dinner at a five-star restaurant) and a layover in Paris. Now, how much of that went to compassion?

Jack, no man is an island. If you view the world with a sense of compassion and are sensitive to the lives of the people in it, then you might be able to do some good from time to time. And you will be a better man for it.

But a sense of reality helps. Sen. Kennedy proclaims his "care for the world" and wants to finance his concerns with *your tax dollars*. And all the while, *his own family* members die of drug overdoses. Swell. Sen. Cranston ran around "caring about people" while his own son was a drug addict. Swell.

So, Jack, be compassionate. Care for others, other than yourself and your own circle of friends. But *start there*, and always consider your motives. Don't be hypocritical or "do for show." Look for those times that you can do some good when nobody else will know.

Realize you have had so many advantages. That's not a reason to feel guilty and do out of guilt. It just puts it in perspective.

Care, my son, you'll be a better man for it.

Love

Dad

2/3/95

Dear Jack,

Congratulations on beating Thacher Wednesday, and congratulations on your goal!! The fact that it puts you in the tournament must be some kind o' satisfaction. I'll see you Saturday for that game.

Let's talk about that rare skill . . . LISTENING:

You will deal with lots and lots of people during your lifetime. It is important to *listen* to what they have to say. You listen for content, obviously, but there is more to listening than just for content.

To really listen, you have to be conscious of the body language that goes with the content. Look at their eyes, do they make contact? That's usually a sign of sincerity and being relaxed. Do they shift foot to foot or squirm? A sign of nervousness; why? Do they lean forward to get closer? A sign of trying to persuade or impress. Do they lean away or back away? That's a sign of negativeness or rejection. Some cultures (i.e., Mediterranean) tend to want to be closer than, say, Northern Europeans as they converse . . . arms crossed across the chest is a sure sign of negative feelings.

Jack, there are lots of signs in body language. *Learn them.* But mostly, *be aware that they exist* and *listen to them* along with the words.

Besides the content and the body language that goes with it, the words themselves reveal. Listen to the words.

Listen for accents. That will tell you where a person is from. That's an easy one.

Listen to the words themselves:

People who use words like "classy," "my old lady," "bosses," "big dough," etc., are from lower-class backgrounds. Other word usage will tell you about a person's experience: A man who uses the phrase "the joint" has been in jail; a man who says "the coast" is from the East or Midwest; a man who refers to San Francisco as "the city" is usually upper-class from the West; a man who calls it "Frisco" is very ordinary and never lived there.

Listen for jargon, cult words, insider words. They are a sign of insecurity, pretentiousness, or just silliness. i.e.: The jargon words of educators ("underachieve" or "physically challenged") that can't speak straight because they can't *think straight*. i.e.: The alphabet soup of the bureaucrats. ("Get your 1099 to the IRS before you apply for a title 9 to HUD or we'll give you a section 8, PDQ.") They can't really think like that, can they? Answer: Yes!! i.e.: The cult words of the computer or stereo "techies." i.e.: The "in words" of the hunters or divers or fishermen or political consultants or some business types.

Usually, people that use jargon words, cult words, and insider terms are insecure and showing off. They ain't really trying to communicate, other than *their* worth, which they ain't really sure of!!

Listen for the manufactured words of the intellectually lazy. My favorite is "doable." There are a million more I can't think of at the moment.

Listen for artificial language that denotes nervousness and/or insecurity. i.e.: Throwing the listener's name randomly into sentences. i.e.: Saying, "At this point in time" (for "now") or "Let the record show" or "I'm someone that believes that" or "As I'm sure you already know . . ." (Well, if I know it, why repeat it?) Such pretensions and affectations are plain bullshit!

Listen for the clichés of the intellectually lazy, pretentious, or just plain BS artists: "Behind closed doors"; "a very private . . ." (either it's private or it's not); "in high places" (like the 4th floor); "at headquarters" (Ugh!!).

And son, as you listen to others, realize that *others are listening to you*.

Speak succinctly, clearly, and without affectations, jargon, or "buzz words." Avoid physical gestures unless you *use* them to make a point. Use words that your listener will understand.

Jack, listening can be fun and if you do it well, it's a powerful tool. Speaking is fun, effective, and a powerful tool, *if you do it well*.

The name of the game is *communication*, so do it!! And do it well.

> Love
>
> Dad

. . . Someday soon I'll tell you about jokes, stories, and using quotes and literary references in communication. . . . They are fun.

2/12/95

Dear Jack,

I just received your grades and teacher comments. Thanks for calling me last week with the preview.

Well, old boy, you've come a long way since your freshman year! One day we'll have to go back and compare teacher comments year to year. You'll be able to trace your growth in maturity, intellect, and general academic deportment.

In a word, I couldn't be more proud of you. . . ."Each and every day I see improved comprehension," "Understands complex & abstract ideas," "Enjoys challenging himself," "I could not be more pleased". . . physics. "A very capable mathematics student," "Produces high quality work," "Is interested and attentive". . . math. "Has worked steadily, cheerfully & effectively," "Throws himself into [the subject]," "I've enjoyed his spirit & enthusiasm". . . English. "Serious and committed," "Accepts full responsibility for meeting challenges". . . art history.

Your Spanish teacher wants you to speak up more . . . Do it. Your math teacher says you are sometimes late. . . . Huh!?! "Late to class". . . Jack, give me a break. This is a new one!

Clearly, Jack, you don't test well. This has been a problem for a long time and one you need to address with more seriousness. You can add a half a grade point or so just by learning the techniques of testing better.

Your grades (3 B's—2 A's), doing all honors and AP classes at Cate School, ain't bad . . . It's not great, but it sure ain't bad. You can pull it up at least to 3 A's and 2 B's, or maybe even better, by the end of the year. So do it.

Bonning's comments were extraordinary. You should be very proud to be so highly thought of . . . same for Dennison's comments. I really don't think those comments were Yak Butter, I think they really meant it!!

Anyway, congratulations. Don't let up! Do your very best in these final three months of your Cate career.

Love

Dad

2/19/95

Dear Jack,

A foursome teed off this morning on the golf course at the base of Mt. Suribachi, 700 miles S/E of the Japanese mainland, on an obscure island in the Bonin Group. The Japanese golfers played their game on a 5,120-acre island that a volcano created less than a century ago: Iwo Jima.

Fifty years ago, 70,000 of your fellow Americans stormed the shores of that tiny island to take it away from the Japanese and clear the way for the invasion of Japan.

That's 50 years ago today!

The casualty rate in that amphibious invasion was over 95% and it took thirty-six days and 20,000 Japanese soldiers killed before five of our marines erected the American flag on Mt. Suribachi. I'm sure you've seen the famous picture of that momentous event, bought by the lives and blood of so many.

This afternoon a friend of mine stopped by to show off his new Mitsubishi sports car. Incidentally, that company is the same company that made the Japanese "Zero," their best World War II fighter plane. I was appalled!!

Yesterday, the Clinton administration announced a record American trade deficit, the greatest portion of which relates to our imbalance with Japan. It amounts to some $40 or $50 billion (that's with a B) a year.

So, you say, what's all this mean and who cares what happened on some little bitty island half a world away, a half a century ago? Hell, that's almost prehistoric to a man of eighteen!!

Well, old boy, I'll tell you . . . I was just 4½ that day 50 years ago and I can remember it to this day. Your grandfather was an intelligence officer, home on leave, and he told your grandmother and me it was the prelude to the invasion of Japan and we would lose "a million of our boys in that effort." I really didn't understand, but I could tell that he was serious as hell.

We were at war with the country that pulled the sneak attack on Pearl Harbor. You have visited the Pearl Harbor Memorial and stood over the watery grave of 1,200 victims of that Japanese attack . . . and we had to finish them off.

The atomic bomb made the job a lot easier and far less costly. (But now the liberal academics at the Smithsonian would have you believe *America* was somehow at fault and poor little Japan was "just trying to preserve its unique culture.")

Well, old boy, the war with Japan goes on today. We're in Phase II and it's an economic battle this time. No bullets . . . dollars and yen. But make no mistake it's war to the death!! And they are serious as a heart attack!

First they targeted us, industry by industry: Cameras (remember Kodak?), sewing machines (remember Singer?), machine tools (remember Massy-Ferguson?), T.V.s (remember Zenith and RCA?), bicycles (remember Schwinn?), motorcycles (remember Harley almost went under?), and electronics and then autos. They used cartel tactics (called *Karitsue* in Japan) that are illegal "restraint of trade" here, and they beat us at the capitalism we perfected.

So now we ship $40–50 billion a year to the Japanese and find them buying some of American's premier companies with our own money (i.e., MCA, Columbia, etc.) and we find that the five biggest banks in the world are Japanese. They even own the Bank of California . . . . How's that for a home-state insult?

While we can't ship our superior, cheaper beef or oranges to them and Motorola is locked out of their cellular market and Boone Pickens can't buy a seat on the board of one of their auto parts companies, they laugh their ass off at how dumb and soft we are!!

And our government does nothing!!

And you ask how this could happen? . . . The Japanese have hired nine of the last ten American trade representatives to work for *them*. They spend $500,000,000 a year on *American lobbyists* to help them beat America. That's how it has happened . . . under both Republican *and* Democrat administrations.

So why do I tell you all this on the 50th anniversary of Iwo Jima?

Because you are an American and your country is at war. We've talked about the drug war. Now I've introduced you to the trade war.

You are free and an American. As Americans have been called upon before to sacrifice and defend their country (i.e., on Iwo Jima), you too may be called upon to fight a war to preserve your freedom and be able to pass it on to your son. . . . *Liberty ain't free, Jack.*

Now, just understand. Later you must be prepared to fight for your country.

     Love

        Dad

2/21/95

Dear Jack,

Your call last night disturbed me a lot. You sounded so down. When you said your social life was "the pits" and your academic life was "a grind" I could picture a very unhappy guy. . . . Jack, you've been hit with a disease called "Senioritis." You're a "short-termer" and it shows.

In reality, you've gotten about as much *out of* Cate as you could and put about as much *into* Cate as you could. Psychologically, old boy, you're gone!! You're ready to move on.

A couple of points:

1. There are only *fourteen weeks until you graduate*!!! . . . And two of those weeks are spring break!! And you know that the last two weeks will be all senior activities. So, bottom line is that all you really have to endure is *10 more weeks*!!

2. Again I remind you that races are won in the final 3 or 4 meters and games are won or lost in the final seconds. You will be remembered to a great degree by your *last* impressions. So don't let down, *kick to the finish*! Demonstrate your real character by holding together to the final day. A lot of your colleagues won't, so you will stand out even more . . . and have the personal satisfaction of knowing you finished well.

As you know, Steph was here for the three-day weekend. We did the blossom trail and it was magnificent!!

Saturday I took her to a clogging convention (!?!?!) down at the Holiday Plaza. She had never seen clogging and I told her about its origin in Ireland and Scotland and how it developed in the "hollows" of the Appalachian Mountains among the 18th century settlers. The people were pretty unattractive and she wasn't impressed.

Jack, you won't believe Steph when next you see her. In the past two or three weeks it seems that she has grown up a year or so . . . *boom*!! It's not just that she has her bands off and seems to have grown two inches . . . it's much more than that. She's different, more mature, more a young lady.

Some of the stories she tells about Derek and his moodiness and lack of social life and lack of ethics and almost total preoccupation with his computer worry me a lot. But there is not much I can do. How different he is than you were at fifteen and how different his world is than yours was at that age. . . . You were very lucky, and *you* made the most of it.

A word about perspective. You should ponder for a moment the incredible age in which you live.

When I was in Washington in the late '70s, I met a crusty old congressman named Claude Pepper. On his wall was a signed picture of Wilbur Wright and alongside of it, one of Neil Armstrong. (I had dinner with Armstrong once.) . . . Just think, a man who knew the pilot of the first airplane *and* the first man to land on the moon, 65 or so years later.

Think of all that has occurred in *your* lifetime, let alone that of your dad. And think of all that will come in the years ahead . . . developments in medicine, science, communications, computers, transportation, etc., etc., etc. And you will be there to *see it* and, more than that, you will be *prepared to benefit* from each of the developments to come. *How lucky you are.* What a wonderful time to be alive and young.

OK, sport, ten weeks to go, then a great summer. <u>NEXT STOP: COLLEGE !!</u>

I love you, Jack,

Dad

P.S. Oh yes . . . who do you want to invite to your graduation? Jeff Reese wants an invite, as does Lonnie. (How many people do you get to invite?) . . . Let me know. . . .

Dad

3/6/95

Dear Jack,

It rained last night & this morning the fog had settled in. About an hour ago the sun broke through and it's now a glorious morning. The flowers are blooming all over the yard and the birds are back. I'm at the dining room table working and having my coffee and you wouldn't believe the sight outside the window at the bird feeder: There are about a hundred birds; blue jays, doves, blackbirds, wild canaries, swallows, a couple of mockingbirds, and some of those funny little birds that hang on the wall. You wouldn't believe it. . . . Amazing! Spring is here!!

I read something last night that resonates truth and a bit of wisdom: *Little* people focus on *people*, *average* people focus on *things*, *big* people focus on *ideas*. Think about it. T.V.: *Hard Copy* vs. A&E. Magazines: *People* vs. *National Review*. People: The gossips vs. people of ideas. Books: O.J. Simpson's vs. Bill Bennett's. Think of the people we know who can only talk about others (fortunately *few*), the people we know who think and talk about things all the time, and the people we know who can read about and talk about ideas for hours at a time. It may be appropriate to ask yourself from time to time where you would calibrate yourself on this spectrum.

Jack, you are learning something some men don't learn until much later, and some not at all: Women can *really bend a man's head around if the man lets it happen*. The dilemma is that if you really *engage* yourself with a woman, you leave yourself vulnerable to *precisely* what you are now going through with Beth. The only way to really ensure that this kind of emotional trauma never happens to you is to never *really* be emotionally involved. And that of course denies you the real joy of a relationship. Thus, the dilemma!!

You'll have to decide for yourself how much you will give & trust again.

I just realized that if I post this letter today it probably will get to you Saturday and, of course, you will have left for spring break. So you won't get it until after you return to school. Oh well, I'll mail it anyway and you'll have a letter waiting for you. Joy.

That's it for now.

Love

Dad

4/20/95

Dear Jack,

Congratulations!! Invitations for admission from Cal, UCLA, and the USC honors program *isn't exactly shabby*. Jack, you should be proud of yourself and all the hard work you have put in to arrive at this position. I'm certainly proud of you. You set out four years ago to gain a first-rate secondary education and to be admitted to a first-rate western university. You've accomplished both. (And had a pretty good time in the process.)

Now comes the decision as to which university best fits your needs and abilities and which university you can make the greatest contribution to. Cal, UCLA, and USC each have unique personalities, strengths, and weaknesses. But, you couldn't go wrong choosing any one of them. And besides, you will get out of college pretty much what you put into it, so any one of them will be good for Jack Broome.

This will be a big decision for you. I think you ought to talk it over with some of your teachers and a couple of alums of each school. Think about where you want to spend the next four years and which school will best prepare you for graduate school.

You have a couple of weeks to decide, so relax, take a breath, and savor your success before plowing into the decision process. . . . Anyway, we'll talk about it more during Parents' Weekend. I'm anxious to hear your opinions.

Can you believe that this weekend will be your eighth, *and last*, Parents' Weekend?!? Well, old boy, *I* can't believe it! It seems like just yesterday that I dropped you off at Savage House and six weeks later was our *first* Parents' Weekend. . . . Time has passed so quickly, yet so much has occurred and you have grown up so much.

Jan will be up Friday morning to attend classes with you and I'll drive down as soon as I pick Steph up. We'll get there about 7:30 and we can all go out to dinner to celebrate your college admissions. We'll stay over to Sunday, but I'll have to leave by 1:30 in order to get Steph back to her mother's by 6:00.

Now then, just seven weeks of school to go. . . . Don't let senioritis get you!! A lot of kids fall apart once they get their college admissions. They let down, blow their grades, and leave lasting memories of being a "screw-up." Jack, remember the old show business saying: "You're only as good as your last act"? And this last seven weeks at Cate is the culmination of your Cate career, your "last act.". . . Go out in style!!

That's it for now. Again, congratulations!!

Love

Dad

4/27/95

Dear Jack,

I left Cate Sunday with a lot of mixed emotions: The weekend with you, Jan, and Steph was a lot of fun. I was proud of your maturity, the way you played in your tennis match, and the fact that you have kept your grades up. I enjoyed our walk on the beach.

Jack, I agree with your choice of USC. Cal Berkeley is certainly a fine school. But it's a mob scene, the class choices are strained at best; the atmosphere is liberal to the extreme; lower division classes are huge and/or taught by T.A.s; the highly touted professors are preoccupied with their "publish or perish" world; and the social life leaves a lot to be desired. Were you headed for a career in the sciences, mathematics, or engineering, I'd say, "U.C.," but as a liberal arts / business major, I don't think Cal is the place for you. The same goes pretty much for UCLA but the social life is better, it's not as dirty, and it's not quite as much of a zoo.

USC is quite different. It is more conservative, has a great social life (almost *too much*), it's very business oriented (its business school is ranked 5th in the country in entrepreneurship), the alumni association is very strong, you'll be going to school with a lot of middleclass kids like yourself, and, in the honors program, your education will be first-rate. So you have my blessing and support. I think you made a good choice.

Frankly, Jack, I'm glad you chose to go to a western school. Were you to have gone east you might have been caught up in the East Coast–oriented culture, married an East Coast girl, and been tempted to go with an East Coast business. There is a lot to be said for the East, and the Midwest, for that matter, but you are a Californian, you speak Spanish, your personal culture is western, and there is plenty of time to go east . . . perhaps for graduate school. . . . Besides, I'll see you a hell of a lot more at USC than if you were at Yale or Columbia or BU or Georgetown. Anyway, you're in for a great next four years.

     Love

       Dad

5/10/95

Dear Jack,

Well, this is it, old boy. You're winding up your Cate career and you graduate in just two weeks. WOW! Has it sunk in yet? I mean *really* sunk in?

I keep thinking about how hard you worked to gain acceptance to Cate and then how happy we were when the letter came. And then, four long, yet so short, years ago, you and I drove up the hill and moved you into Savage House. You were a little kid of fourteen, trying to be so confident, yet kind of scared inside. (But only you and I knew that, and I'm not sure you knew that *I* knew.)

And now four years have passed. *You* are the senior, graduating and going off to college, that you saw and looked up to four years ago.

You bore down on your studies, competed with very bright kids with solid primary school foundations, and now you are graduating with a 3.9 GPA and have been accepted into the honors program at USC.

You completed the full course of mathematics, from algebra to advanced placement calculus. You took United States, European, and Asian history. You took four years of Spanish, from basic grammar to advanced literature, and spent a summer in Spain, living with a Spanish family and attending the University of Salamanca. You did the sciences, physics and chemistry. You mastered the English language from grammar to speech to poetry to literature. You gained some culture with art history, photographic composition, and music appreciation and attended symphonies and operas. You have wonderful teachers that taught you and inspired you and gave you a love of learning. A couple of them pissed you off and several became real friends. You studied until 3:00 A.M. often, learned a real facility with computers, and learned academic discipline. You met deadlines, learned to follow instructions, and had the satisfaction of many jobs well done.

You earned a varsity letter in your freshman year and then lettered in three sports: lacrosse, soccer, and tennis. Your teams won your league and you played in national lacrosse tournaments. And you captained your tennis team. You learned to surf on weekends and mountain biked the Santa Barbara peaks. Over these past four years you grew nine inches, put on fifty pounds, and, at 18, you are a strapping six footer (give or take a half inch).

You've made wonderful, lifelong friends among the seven Cate classes that attended school with you. You've been invited to homes in northern and southern California, Las Vegas and Singapore, a summer cottage on Lake Geneva, and a ranch in Montana. You've made friends by being a friend. You are a leader and a role model at Cate and when you leave you will be missed. Your sense of humor has lightened many moments, your character and values have inspired your classmates.

The challenges you have faced at Cate have taught you about yourself. You have learned to use your strengths and you have learned how to compensate for your weaknesses. You have learned that you aren't a great test-taker and that you need to gain skills in that area. You have found that your lack of political correctness can cost you in some quarters and that you will have to deal with it. You have learned, in a highly concentrated setting, how you relate to a wide variety of people and personalities.

You have been true to the values you brought to Cate and during the last four years you have used and refined those values. You grew up at Cate. The little boy of four years ago is a man now.

You can be very proud of yourself and your Cate career. I am!!

But Jack, the job of growing a *really great* Jack Broome isn't done. You are just fourteen weeks from starting your *college* career. I promise you that the next four years will be the most fun and exhilarating years of your life. And you are well prepared for it. You can enter college with confidence.

Your little pond is about to become a big lake, Jack. You will meet and learn from world-class minds. You will be exposed to new ideas and concepts that now you can't even imagine. You will use the knowledge and skills you gained at Cate to ascend to new heights personally and intellectually. You will develop your intellectual curiosity and reflectiveness. You will learn to speak publicly with greater facility (not one of your present strengths). I hope you will develop a greater ability to express your real feelings and not bottle them up so much inside yourself (again, not one of your present strengths). You will start college with broad "survey" courses and then narrow your focus more and more to the areas of your real interests and future life's work.

Your education will become more and more practical and useful for your life's career.

And your social life will be wonderful. Fun guys, a variety of friends, and dating beautiful, athletic women, will be your distraction every day (and night). You'll have a ball. . . . And you've earned it!

So, Jack, savor these last two bittersweet weeks at Cate. You'll *never* forget Cate and what you became there. And you will return for alumni functions for the next fifty years. (That's to the year 2045!!!) And with each year, your time at Cate will mean more and more to you and you will realize more and more what you got out of these last four years. And you will also remember what *you gave Cate*. And that will mean a lot, too.

So during these last two weeks go around to each of your teachers and thank them for their contributions to your life. And thank your friends for their friendship and what they have meant to you. . . . Don't assume "that they know" how you feel (as you often do). They don't. *Tell them.*

There will be a big temptation to cut loose and have a "belt" or two. *Don't!* There will be a temptation to lower your standards academically and socially. *Don't!* Stay a class act and you will be *even more so* in the doing.

So, Jack, enjoy these last two weeks, *do what's right*, and we'll see you at graduation. (I'll be the one with tears in his eyes and a very proud look on his face, because his son always did his very best.)

Love

Dad

December 28, 1994

I am delighted to write a letter of recommendation for Jack
Broome, whom I got to know well when I was headmaster of Cate
School.

Jack is simply a first-rate human being. On the one hand, he is
kind-hearted, modest, even-keeled - a young man who thoroughly
enjoys other people and really cares about them; on the other, he
is deeply, even passionately, committed to his principles and
firmly holds to them, often in contrast to his self-serving
fellow adolescents. This balance of affability and conviction,
plus outstanding academic and athletic accomplishment, have made
him one of the top students, leaders, and, most importantly,
people at Cate School this year.

In his dormitory Jack really knows what it is going on, spends a
lot of time insuring that things run smoothly, and is a terrific
role model. His leadership, example, and behind-the-scenes
counselling have contributed significantly to the positive
feeling of community both in his dormitory and in the school as a
whole. And Jack himself is capping off a steady personal growth
in the process: to his intrinsic goodness he has added poise,
increasing force, and altogether appealing self-assurance.

Jack has always been an earnest, diligent, and keenly interested
student. His teachers compliment his genuine interest in
learning, and his academic record is a solid and impressive
refection of his fine ability. Jack's advisor last year
described his development as "reaching the point of being one of
the finest young scholars in his class, and his being recognized
as one of the most talented students in the school by his
teachers."

Jack's talent and leadership is also abundantly obvious in
athletics. A skilled and competitive athlete, Jack anchored the
defense on the soccer team this year; he is one of the returning
lettermen who will be critical to Cate's success in lacrosse; and
he will, again this year, be integral to continuing the School's
extraordinary success in tennis. Cate was undefeated last year
until the semi-finals of the California Interscholastic

Federation playoffs last year, and they should be equally
competitive this year. Jack has a great attitude in athletics,
and, in many ways, exemplifies the very best qualities of the
athlete in team sports. He is dedicated, unselfish, skillful -
at once the spirit of the team, a fine sportsman, and an
exceptional performer.

I admire Jack Broome for his integrity, his firm loyalty to his
many friends and to his school, and his determination to do his
best as a student and as a leader. He is the type of young man
that one likes immensely because he is so good in all ways.

While Jack recognizes full well how competitive admission into
          he is, nevertheless, determined to attend, and I
recommend him enthusiastically as the kind of young man who can
and will make a difference.

                              Sincerely,

                              Scott McLeod
                              Headmaster

bc: John Broome

SHAW STEEL STRUCTURES, INC.

GENERAL BUILDING CONTRACTORS • METAL BUILDING ERECTORS

September 20, 1994

Mr. Jack C. Broome

Dear Mr. Broome,

I would like to take a few minutes to commend you for the exceptional performance of your duties within our corporation during the summer of 1994. We like to appropriately recognize those individuals who are truly outstanding employees. Your willing attitude, eagerness to learn, acceptance of instructions, and friendly smile is truly exceptional.

Your position with Shaw Steel Structures, Inc. performing all phases of steel construction and metal building erection was unfailingly dependable. We do appreciate the effort that you have given your position within our firm and feel that the efficiency with which you perform will carry over into all future endeavors.

You have provided excellent service and proved to always be dependable during your employment. Your commitment to providing the highest possible level of service is unsurpassed. You have given an excellent example of those qualities we portray to our clients and with those examples, we feel confident that those, our clients, will return for future needs. This is the basis of our client relations and without people like you to fulfill our promise of quality, we would be unable to continue the success that we have achieved.

Again, we thank you for your dedication and reliability during your employment with us and would like to express our desire to employ you again should the future provide this opportunity.

Best Wishes,

Paul W. Shaw/Mildred L. Shaw
Shaw Steel Structures, Inc.

Recommendation for Jack Broome

Since coming to Cate School as a ninth - grader, Jack Broome has distinguished himself as an extremely popular and highly capable young man, whose record of achievement extends across a broad range of interests. Jack is a fine student, a versatile athlete and an increasingly influential member of the community. His personal qualities have had much to do with his success here, and perhaps most notable among these are his unwavering integrity ,his loyalty to others, his seriousness of purpose and the sense of pure fun which he brings to everything he does.

Indeed, the combination of his "joie de vivre" and personal integrity is an essential characteristic of Jack's nature, and it seems to lift the spirits of those around him, no matter what the task at hand. He contributes by doing everything from cleaning bathrooms in dormitory to taking time out of his busy schedule to have a heart-to-heart conversation with an underclassmen who is having difficulty at Cate. He doesn't talk about leadership, he exemplifies leadership. In short, what gives such a pleasant edge to Jack's leadership is that he sees life as something to enjoy to the fullest and he refuses to let disappointments affect him for long. Despite his ability to see the humor in just about anything, including himself, he is always very serious about and more concerned with doing good and doing well.

Although Jack is well-liked for his charm and personality, his peers know that there is much more to him that. He is an intelligent, insightful fellow, and he is regularly sought out for his opinions on matters relating to student life here at Cate. He gets along easily with all sorts of people, and he has become one of the leaders of the senior class, despite the fact that he has chosen no such official position. He's very open-minded, his instincts are good, and he treats others with considerable sensitivity; as a consequence he has come to wield significant influence among the student body.

Jack's classwork reflects the same combination of ability and enthusiasm we have described. He really loves to learn , and his academic performance in all subjects, including a number of honors level and advanced placement courses, has been consistently excellent . He has also earned solid scores on all his national exams, although I don't feel the scores reflect the excellent work Jack has done at Cate.

Allow me to paraphrase what some of Jack's teachers say about him: In Spanish, his teacher comments that Jack's writing in Spanish approximates that of a native speaker-- he studied a whole summer in an immersion program in Spain. Other comments about his work throughout his career include : " Jack is a perceptive reader , and his writing is clean, clear, always to the point " (English 11) ; "He has an excellent aptitude in math, as indicated by his ease in learning and applying new concepts" (Pre-calculus) ; and finally, "Jack responds well to criticism, takes all suggestions to heart, and works carefully at learning from his mistakes" (History). In short, Jack has been called the most disciplined student at Cate School by students and faculty, alike.

On the playing fields, Jack is a versatile athlete. He is a varsity letter winner in soccer, lacrosse, and tennis(where he is captain of the team). He is strong, fast, and very fit, to start with, and he complements these physical attributes with good instincts and an almost legendary work ethic. He is a winner. He has a keen sense of sportsmanship, but he is also aggressive and just reckless enough to raise the intensity of any contest in which he participates. And he has indeed participated in many athletic contests during his years here. His drive and determination, combined with a history of coming through in the clutch, have earned him a tremendous respect from both his teammates and competitors.

I have watched Jack Broome mature into one of the most popular and most widely respected members of his class. In a period of transition at Cate, he has been one of the student leaders who has been the glue in keeping his class focused , together, and positive. If Stanford is looking for someone who may have a positive and profound affect on those around him as well as the world, it should not flinch in accepting Jack to the Class of 1999.

Sincerely,

Albert R. Cauz
Instructor of Spanish
Phillips Academy
Andover, M